PRAISE FOR *HONOURING OUR KID[*

"Nola Peacock is an absolutely amazing person and coach. In my life, I have to shut down and to never fully trust anyone, but Nola has helped me to open up and be vulnerable while still feeling safe, something I've never been able to do. I have always struggled with confidence and my self-worth, but Nola has helped me to begin to see myself as I *truly* am, free of the messages and false beliefs that have been engrained into my mind, and by extent lead a more fulfilling life enveloped in the feeling that I do matter. On more than one occasion, Nola has helped me to get through moments when I felt I couldn't do 'it' anymore and felt that ending my life was the answer. I would recommend Nola with all my heart as a coach for any and all ages and any and all reasons. She is kind, comforting, and holds the innate gift to help you accomplish what you never thought you could and to work through things you thought were eternal. Thank you Nola!"

—**Madeline Clark,** client, age 19

"This book literally changed the way I parent and helped me to see my kids and role as a parent in a completely new way. It's led me to a much more fulfilling and peaceful relationship with my kids and has given me the most precious thing all parents yearn for: genuine connection with their kids. Thank you, Nola, for creating such a compelling perspective on parenting *and* for the easy-to-follow steps to create real and lasting change for parents and kids."

—**Karen McGregor,** international speaker and best-selling author

"As I read this book, I felt listened to as a parent. In turn, Nola reminds us that the most important thing our kids need from us is to be listened to. Nola Peacock brings her considerable professional background to the writing of this sensitive, uplifting book for parents.

"With remarkable insight and generosity, she recounts some of her own most painful times and how she was comforted by what she learned from others. I'm glad she is passing this wisdom on to readers and showing us how we can apply it to our own parenting experiences."

—**Kitty Raymond,** founder, Raymond Parenting

"Nola's book is on my list of 'books worth reading more than once.' As a father, paediatrician, life coach, and a marathon runner, I am acutely aware of how hard it is to always honour our kids. Nola brings much-needed light and healing through her book, and as a former nurse, she is skilled in navigating the emotions of high-needs families—she is superbly credible."

—**Dr. Peter Nieman,** FRCP (C), FAAP, paediatrician, author, life coach

"Nola Peacock has an amazing gift in being able to support the challenges and the conversations that are happening between parents and their children in today's world. This book has the wisdom, the guidance, and the practical insights parents need to navigate the journey differently, thus creating a better relationship for all involved. I am so grateful to have had her work influence in my life and my wife's life, and the manner in which it has impacted our three beautiful sons is truly incredible. If you are looking to become a better parent and take your family relationships to the next level, you must read this book."

—Trevor McGregor, Peak Performance Results Coach,
The Anthony Robbins Group of Companies

"If you're a parent who wants to connect deeply with your children, this is an excellent book with practical tips on raising emotionally healthy and independent children."

—Renaye Thornborrow, CEO, Adventures in Wisdom Inc.

HONOURING OUR KIDS

HONOURING OUR KIDS

HOW TO ENCOURAGE
GROWING HEARTS & MINDS

NOLA PEACOCK

Advantage®

Published by Advantage, Charleston, South Carolina.
Member of Advantage Media Group.

ADVANTAGE is a registered trademark, and the Advantage colophon is a trademark of Advantage Media Group, Inc.

Printed in the United States of America.

ISBN: 978-1-59932-718-1
LCCN: 2016962294

Cover design by Katie Biondo.

Names and identifying details have been changed to protect the privacy of individuals.

This publication is designed to provide accurate and authoritative information in regard to the subject matter covered. It is sold with the understanding that the publisher is not engaged in rendering legal, accounting, or other professional services. If legal advice or other expert assistance is required, the services of a competent professional person should be sought.

 Advantage Media Group is proud to be a part of the Tree Neutral® program. Tree Neutral offsets the number of trees consumed in the production and printing of this book by taking proactive steps such as planting trees in direct proportion to the number of trees used to print books. To learn more about Tree Neutral, please visit **www.treeneutral.com.**

Advantage Media Group is a publisher of business, self-improvement, and professional development books. We help entrepreneurs, business leaders, and professionals share their Stories, Passion, and Knowledge to help others Learn & Grow. Do you have a manuscript or book idea that you would like us to consider for publishing? Please visit **advantagefamily.com** or call **1.866.775.1696.**

To Ryan & Christa
Thank you for blessing my life every single day

TABLE OF CONTENTS

ACKNOWLEDGEMENTS

First, I would like to thank my parents for their love, support, and all they have taught me. Thank you to Erin, Mark, Jeff, Fred, Anthony, and many other young souls who are no longer with us. You changed my perspective on what is truly important in life and how precious life is. I want to thank my son, Ryan, and my daughter, Christa, for teaching me how to be a better parent every day. To my beautiful daughter Sabrina, I thank you for the brief time you were in my life. Losing you taught me the importance of being nonjudgmental and loving unconditionally. Thank you to my clients for being so open and honest and teaching me so much.

I would also like to express my gratitude to all the wonderful people at Advantage Media who have helped make my dream of being an author become reality. You held my hand every step of the way, and I am truly grateful.

ABOUT THE AUTHOR

Nola Peacock, RN, Certified Life Mentor Practitioner, kids' confidence coach, parenting expert, and Reiki master, is passionate about empowering families to gain confidence, improve communication, and have better emotional control so that they can make wiser decisions, reduce power struggles, and actually have fun together. As a mother of two amazing children, ages seventeen and twenty-six, she is very aware of how quickly the time passes before kids are independent and out on their own. She strongly believes that the short time parents have with their children needs to be enjoyed. Nola has heard many parents share their regrets of not spending more time with their kids, and she truly wants to make parenting easier and more fun so that families can create joyful memories together.

Whether parents are looking to reduce the conflict between themselves and their teen, build a stronger connection with their child, or just make parenting easier and more fun, Nola's tested-and-proven advice and exercises that fill the pages of her debut book, *Honouring Our Kids*, will help parents to welcome those results and gain tools to lead the life they envision for themselves and their families. Best of all, parents learn to take care of themselves, feel more confident in their parenting, and empower their children to reach their full potential. Parents cannot give their children self-confidence, resilience, or happiness, but they can guide their children to develop these qualities.

This is why Nola created the Confident Happy Kids and Confident Happy Parents programs. Nola is on a mission to empower and inspire families to create harmonious, nurturing, and loving homes, and her work in the field recently won her a Womanition SuPEARLative Award for education and mentorship.

WHAT OUR KIDS REALLY NEED

My connection with kids comes so naturally that my career as a kids' confidence coach feels almost as though it chose me, rather than the reverse. I've always had an effortless rapport with children and teens; even in high school, I preferred babysitting over going to parties. It was when I started teaching piano at sixteen that I realized a lot of my young students came mainly because they wanted to talk to me about their personal lives and concerns, with me offering them guidance when I could. I never advertised, put up a brochure, or anything like that; I depended solely on word of mouth for new pupils, yet often I had more than I could handle.

When I went into nursing, I knew that I wanted to work with kids. My first job was in pediatric oncology, an experience that really opened my eyes and changed my perspective on things. I was in my early twenties on the very first Christmas Eve that I had to work, and I remember grumbling about it to a young patient, a girl of about fourteen. Her reply really struck me: "At least you get to go home in the morning." I thought, *Yeah, you're right. I actually don't have anything to complain about.*

Seeing what they went through—the procedures, the pokes and prodding, the chemo and hair loss—taught me to look at things from their perspective. After that, if my patients were grumpy or angry or whatever, I thought, *I don't blame you. I would be grouchy, too, if I was stuck in here and having these things done to me.* I started listening to their complaints instead of trying to cheer them up. I would acknowledge, "Yeah, this is tough right now. This sucks," so that they felt that I heard them and understood rather than just whisking in and telling them, "This will be over really quick" and trying to brush it off. I would agree with them—"Yeah, this is crappy"—because it was. I didn't judge them. I accepted them unconditionally, they felt this acceptance, and in exchange, they gave me their trust. They'd allow me to perform the uncomfortable or frightening procedures that they'd refuse to have done by other nurses. One boy of about fourteen, who was retaining fluids and needed regular abdominal measurements taken, would literally fight off the other nurses when they'd come to his room. But with me, he was totally compliant and calm. It wasn't fun for him, but we had a relationship. He knew that I listened to him and that I cared about and accepted him unconditionally, regardless of how he acted or felt. That made the difference for him.

I became the go-to for the "difficult" patients: the kids the other nurses complained about or found too angry or cranky to deal with. I never saw them that way. In fact, I was glad to take them on because I knew that I could make a difference for them. When the other nurses would use break time to chat together, I'd take a game or a book to a patient's room and read to them or play a game. It was often quiet on the night shift, so we'd make Rice Krispies squares in the washbasin with ingredients I'd bring from home. We would melt the butter and the marshmallows in the microwave and then stir in the Rice Krispies. Sometimes I'd organize games; we used masking tape to tape shapes on the floor and then let the kids throw paper plates from their rooms. If their plate landed in the shapes, they got points. Mostly it was the fun and laughter of throwing the plates that made it worthwhile. It was a break from the dreary routines that let them forget their problems for a little bit.

All the stories in that ward didn't end happily, of course. While many kids did go home, we also lost some of our patients. Sitting there with a child taking his or her last breath makes you think very deeply about what's truly important in life. None of those parents cared about having a big house or driving a pricey car; rather, the important thing was their child and the time they had together. Having the memories of playing with those kids, doing what I could to break up the monotony of their hospital stays by sharing a story or a game, kept me going after they had passed away. Those times were important to me. I can only imagine how important memories like that were to the families.

LIFE THROWS US CURVES—EVEN TO THE YOUNGEST AMONG US.

We simply don't know, day to day, what's coming, and as parents, we need to keep that fact foremost in our minds. So much of parenting can become conflict oriented; it's easy to fall into habits that stifle communication and put distance between us and our kids. Heaven forbid if something were to happen to your children; are you going to look back and think about all the times that you yelled at them over their messy room, or can you look back and go, "Oh, remember when we . . .?"

Many parents that I've talked to say they regret not spending more time with their kids. I don't want to have those regrets, and I don't want other parents to have them either. When you're older, you want to look back and think, *I remember when my kids would blow bubbles in their milk,* because that is the kind of thing that you and your kids will look back on with a smile. To me, that's what's truly important in life. I hear parents complaining about messy rooms or homework, and I do understand—I get drawn into it too, sometimes. But honestly, it's not going to matter five years from now, so why should it matter right now? Perspective is so important.

Perspective is so important.

I know—I lost a daughter, Sabrina, who was stillborn twenty-one years ago. I missed out on her first steps and her first day of school. I had two miscarriages before I was blessed with my daughter, who just turned seventeen. I truly appreciate those special moments, such as hearing her singing in the school choir, when it really hits me: *Oh my goodness, I'm so grateful that I get to do this because I didn't with Sabrina.* That's another reason I'm so passionate about my work.

Both of my kids struggled with depression, so I know what that's like for a mother. When my son went through it and was actually suicidal, I searched and searched for answers. He saw a psychologist, and we worked with school liaisons and a crisis team. Some of it helped, and some of it didn't, so my concern became, "Okay, what can I put in place that works?"

Dealing with people's judgmental attitudes toward what my son was going through didn't help either; in fact, it made it much worse. When he simply could not face going to school every day, he quit going. We went out for dinner one night to celebrate my birthday with family, grandparents, and friends, and one woman at the table berated my son, saying, "You need to be going to school."

To see the devastation in his face was shattering. My marriage had been emotionally abusive, and he had suffered through that, so my intuition told me, *No, he needs to heal from that, and then he'll figure it out.* Now he's graduated from university with a business and marketing degree, and he's just a wonderful young man.

In my work, I help kids struggling with everything from self-esteem issues to depression, and I'm going to talk about how we, as the adults in their world, can help them to grow into the strong, resilient, and capable adults we want them to be.

THERE'S ALWAYS A WAY.

This is something I'm passionate about: helping parents and kids see that there are multiple paths to a happy outcome. We very often think there's only one way to get somewhere, and that's just not so. Realizing that options exist is an empowering idea I want to share with parents and their kids, and in the coming chapters we'll talk about new ways to deal with old challenges. My heart breaks when I hear stories about depressed teens committing suicide. That shouldn't be the only way they see to get out of where they are.

OUR KIDS NEED TO BE LISTENED TO.

As busy adults functioning on multiple levels with conflicting demands coming at us, it's perilously easy to stop hearing our kids when they make what may sound like unreasonable demands or accusations.

Those conversations often start with, "Mom, you never spend time with me." The knee-jerk response many times is, "Yes, I do. Look at all I do for you. I get groceries, and I cook for you and do your laundry; I take you to school, I help you with your homework, and we sit and watch TV together."

But your child isn't looking for a catalogue of all your labours on her behalf. What she's really trying to say is, "I want to go for a walk with you," or "I want to play a game with you." In other words, they want us to be present, free of competing demands for our attention, and wholly in the moment with them. It's hard, but it's so important to hear our kids when they ask us for that.

WE ALL HAVE DIFFERENT THINGS THAT MAKE US FEEL VALUED. DO YOU KNOW WHAT MAKES YOUR CHILD FEEL LOVED?

Whether we long for a touch, a little gift, or a heartfelt compliment, we seek many different kinds of affirmation that we matter and are loved. What makes your child feel loved? For my daughter, she loves being touched. She loves cuddling with me and getting and giving big hugs. She's seventeen years old, but she'll sometimes say, "Mom, I really need a hug." Do you know what your child is asking for when he says, "You never spend time with me"? What he's really saying is, "I don't feel like you care," or "You're not listening." The mom of one child I worked with said, "He says the same thing over and over, and I get tired of listening." I had to ask her, "Have you really heard what he's trying to tell you?" Kids will keep saying the same things over and over unless they feel that you get what their meaning is.

Imagine trying to tell someone about an awful day you're having. You say, "Oh, I'm having a bad day and my dog just threw up all over my carpet," and the other person says, "That's easy to clean up," and moves on. What you feel like saying is, "Wait a minute. You're not hearing that I'm having a really bad day here." You didn't want instructions on carpet cleaning; you wanted validation, something along the lines of, "Oh, that really sucks. That sounds like you're having a rough day."

Once you have had your feelings heard and respected, you can move on because you feel acknowledged. *They heard me. I matter. They took the time and the effort to really understand what I'm trying to say or who I am.*

WHAT DOES YOUR CHILD LOVE AND LONG TO SHARE WITH YOU?

Often, boys around age five love dinosaurs, and that's what they want to talk about (sometimes for what feels like forever). If parents can sit and listen and learn (because they usually know more about it than we do), kids feel like, *Oh yeah, Mom cares. She's interested in what I have to say.* So instead of, "I don't have time. I've got to go make dinner," try saying, "What does a Tyrannosaurus eat?" Show that you honour your children by honouring their interests.

WE ALL WANT TO BE LOVED FOR WHO WE TRULY ARE.

Many of our kids put a lot of energy toward trying to be the person that they think their parents want them to be, and that can be a cause of depression. And they can read us. For example, a father won't always necessarily tell his son, "I want you to play hockey," but if the son can see his dad is a big fan of the sport and spends a lot of time watching and talking about it, he's likely to think, *Hmm . . . maybe if I play hockey, Dad will love me more.* So he'll sign up for hockey, trying to please his father because he loves him and just wants to feel important.

As parents, a scenario like this requires us to allow our kids to be their authentic selves. But unless we are listening, acknowledging, and paying attention to what our kids like to do, it's easy to miss when kids are doing something just to please us. It also requires us to be careful in our response and be ready to say, "I didn't think you really liked hockey."

Our kids find themselves in the position of working to please others ahead of themselves. When they get to school, they want to please their teachers and fit in with their peers, and too often that means putting their own needs and wants in last place. As a sage once said, "We're not in this world to live up to others' expectations, nor are they here to live up to ours." Nowhere is that truer than in the relationship between parent and child, but it's too often overlooked.

PARENTS ARE THE GREATEST INFLUENCERS ON THEIR KIDS—BUT THEY'RE NOT THE ONLY ONES.

Those who are entrusted with teaching and coaching our children need to understand just how much impact they have on their students. That impact can be positive or negative; a respected teacher can literally change a child's life with a word of earned praise at the right moment, making them reassess their abilities and believe in themselves. Sadly, the reverse can happen too; I remember in high school when a teacher made a negative comment about a paper I'd written, and from that day I told myself, *I can't write*. Yet, the previous week he had held one of my papers up as an example to the class because I had done a good job. But I focused on that negative comment. When kids hear negatives with that kind of emotional amplification, how many positives does it take to negate that one negative thing? It was only recently that I started believing that I could, in fact, write.

KIDS LIVE UP TO THE EXPECTATIONS THEY'RE GIVEN.

Multiple studies show that kids live up to the expectations they are given, and that's why it's so important that we encourage kids, focusing on their successes and helping them to believe in themselves.[1] That means that if you don't expect them to do well—if you're telling them, "Math is hard"—then they're going to internalize that as truth, and they're not going to do well. You hear of these miracle stories where somebody believed in a child and it completely changed his or her life's trajectory. As adults, we have this power—and we need to use it wisely.

---

1 Citi Trends Data Bank, *Parental Expectations for Their Children's Academic Attainment*, October 2015, http://www.childtrends.org/?indicators=parental-expectations-for-their-childrens-academic-attainment.

THE RIGHT WORD AT THE RIGHT TIME CAN CHANGE OR EVEN SAVE A LIFE.

When a teacher or a coach sees that a kid is struggling and gives a word of encouragement at the right time, it can make a huge difference and very possibly even save a life. Coaches in particular are not always trained to listen or watch for the kinds of clues I'm talking about in terms of mental health, but they should be. Think of archetypical ballet teachers: martinets, tough, and endlessly demanding of near-inhuman perfection in terms of physical appearance and every detail. That's the way that they were taught, so they continue to teach that way. And, of course, the teacher means well and is working to help her students achieve great things, but you have to look at what this teaching method does to the kids who constantly hear their shortcomings and think, *I'm not good enough*, or *I'm not thin enough*. They can suffer from anorexia or depression because of something the teacher said in class. Given the potential outcomes, you have to wonder if the prize is worth the sacrifice.

We often think that for kids to succeed or excel at something, they need to start at a young age—but that's not always the case. I recently met Michelle Coulter Cameron, who won a gold medal at the 1988 Olympics. She was afraid of the water as a young child and did not start swimming until age thirteen. This shows that there is always a way to excel if someone is passionate about what he or she wants to do.

CAN WE DO BETTER? I BELIEVE WE CAN.

Before we judge those tyrannical dance teachers, it's important to keep in mind that that's the way they were taught. Everyone learns to parent or teach through his or her own experiences as a child. Change isn't going to come on its own; it's up to us to let go of some of our old ideas about what is important and choose to do things differently. After all, in the real world, how many of those kids in ballet class are going to be professional dancers? Only a very select few, and their natural gifts will play a big part in that success. The more likely outcome is that they may become dance teachers themselves, working with young kids. And certainly, no matter what these kids do with their lives, they'll need self-confidence and self-esteem to succeed. What we as teachers, coaches, parents, and therapists should be doing—*must* be doing—is helping kids to grow into kind-hearted, confident, and decent adults. This book is here to help.

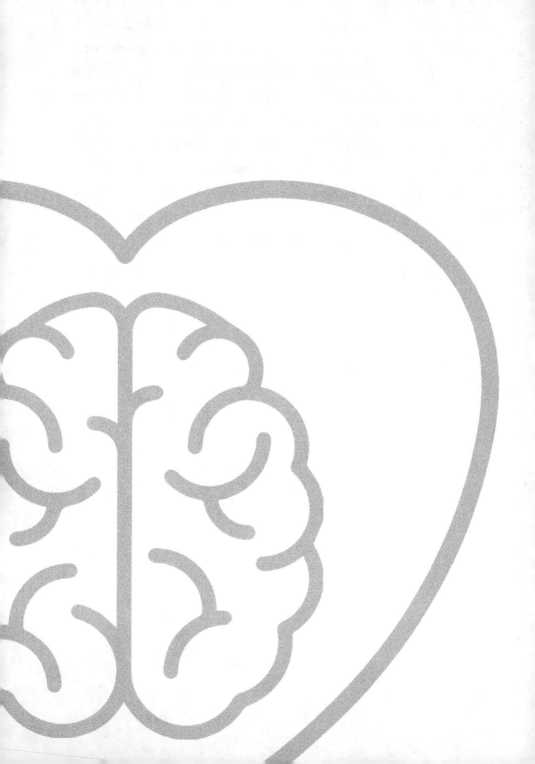

CHAPTER ONE

THE VALUE OF GIVING CHOICES

I mentioned in the introduction the importance of instilling self-esteem in children. If the number of mental-health crises happening on college campuses is an indicator of how we're preparing our children, then this is an area in which we can certainly improve as parents. What, then, should we be doing to develop self-confident kids who are fully prepared for success as young adults? Let's consider the factors.

HELICOPTER KIDS ARE CRASHING AT A FRIGHTENING RATE.

Colleges and universities are reporting that freshmen and sophomores are suffering from so much depression and anxiety that campus healthcare centres are overwhelmed. Many are suggesting this could be linked to the modern tendency to overprotect, overmanage, and overparent—what we call *helicopter parenting*. Overparented kids have no skills for self-care; they're completely at the mercy of whatever is going on around them, especially when they leave home.

I've seen it in my own circle. The mother of one of my son's friends did everything for her son, totally guiding his every step. When the boys were fifteen, the family was going to take my son for a weekend of skiing. The boy's mother phoned me and said, "Here is what he needs to bring. He's going snowboarding. So, he needs his snowboard. He needs his boots. He needs his helmet. He needs clean underwear, a toothbrush . . ."

I could hardly believe it. I thought to myself, *Okay, I must be a bad mom, because he's fifteen years old, and if he forgets something, I guess he'll have to figure it out. I'm not packing for him.* Not surprisingly, when her son went off to university, he crashed and burned. He wound up having to drop out because he couldn't cope with the demands that the new level of independence put on him. Of course, his problems started much earlier than that and are hardly unique.

I work with many parents who struggle to raise independent kids, and homework is a particular problem: "Every night we're doing homework." Epic battles sometimes become a nightly ritual, and I can't help but think how horrible it must be for all concerned to spend every evening fighting over homework.

I don't put up with this type of bickering. If my kids need help, I'm there to help them. But I don't ask them if they have homework, and I don't nag them. I certainly don't tell them how to do it. If I get the sense that they're asking for more help than they need, my response is along the lines of, "I went to school. I did it. You guys can handle your own work." They know I'm always there to support them if they have questions or need supplies. But they understand that doing their homework is not my responsibility—it's theirs.

Homework needs to be between children and their teachers—but that frightens parents because if the kids don't do their homework, there will be consequences, whether in the form of lowered grades or punishments. Somehow, we have gotten the idea that part of our job as parents is sparing our kids the consequences of their choices. I think parents also worry about being judged. If our kids don't do well, do other people—such as their teachers—think we are bad parents?

Even when talking with parents I know personally, often I only hear about the things their kids are doing. I like hearing about other people's kids, but I also want to know what my friends are up to. Parents' lives shouldn't revolve around their kids' lives. They need to have their own passions, friends, and activities.

I'm not suggesting that parents deemphasize the importance of homework. It is important, which is why we can't be forever running interference and rescuing our children from the consequences of irresponsible behaviour. What does that protection teach them that will be useful in adult life, the preparation for which is the whole purpose of parenting?

You have to give the choice back to your child and let her live with the consequences: "Okay, so you chose not to do your homework, and now you have to stay after school and do it or stay in at lunch and do it. That's your choice. Next time, how will you handle it?" Again, this requires listening and talking to your kids and underlining the fact that it's their choice and that the consequences will be theirs, too. Walk them through the steps. Otherwise, how and when will they learn to choose correctly? By the time you send them off to college, it's too late.

LET YOUR KIDS MAKE THEIR OWN CHOICES, AND START THEM YOUNG.

Many of us are constantly telling our kids what to do next, every step of the way. Naturally this leads to resistance and conflicts because nobody really likes being told what to do. More to the point, what you end up with are people who don't know what to do next unless they're told.

It's much better for the family dynamic (and for your kids as future adults) to start giving them opportunities to make their own choices from a very young age. Resist the temptation to grab the wheel; instead, try, "It's up to you." This gives them the opportunity to make mistakes. Start this approach when your children are young because when they're in grade one and don't do their assigned homework, there is not going to be a huge consequence. The teacher may say, "You have to stay in at recess and do this." The next time, they'll do it because they don't want to miss recess. But if you've been telling them all through high school to do their homework, and you sit with them and nag at them and make them do it, then when they get to university or college, there won't be anyone telling them to do their homework, so they won't do it—and the consequences are far more severe. Let them choose, let them make mistakes, and be there to help them if and when they ask for it. Support them—but don't rescue them.

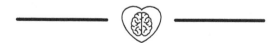

Let them choose, let them make mistakes, and be there to help them if and when they ask for it. Support them—but don't rescue them.

SURVIVING OUR FAILURES MAKES US STRONGER.

Why is it important to let kids make their own mistakes? Because life throws us all curve balls, and we all occasionally mess up. But the good news is that it's not usually fatal; we pay for our mistakes and move on, better and smarter than we were. Making small mistakes builds our resilience and confidence that we are able to handle big things. You can lose your job, experience a death in the family, or have any of a million other upsets, but the question is, how do you navigate through these things?

If kids make mistakes and fail at something, you don't want them to think it's necessarily a tragedy. They need to be able to say, "Okay, I messed up. The world didn't end. How do I get past it?" If parents are doing everything for their kids and never really allowing them to fail or to mess up, then the first time that something does go wrong, those kids have no clue what to do and they panic, thinking there's no way out. This can cause them to become depressed and sometimes even suicidal.

INDEPENDENCE TAKES PRACTICE.

Kids who don't have a real grasp of how their actions create results and who lack a sense of personal power, efficacy, and self-esteem are kids who will struggle to be independent because they've had no practice. I had a client, a boy of fourteen whose parents had a cabin in Ontario. He and his family would visit the cabin at different times. In one instance, his dad and younger brother were going to go out to the cabin, and of course he was invited to go. Normally he would have gone too, but he was conflicted about it. Through the process of the two of us talking through what was really important to him, he made the choice to stay home with his mom so that he could put in some extra time practising his instrument—he was in the marching band, and they were preparing for a big concert event.

At the same time, as this boy and I talked through things, he realized that sometimes his friends would invite him to go out and he would say, "no" because he felt like he needed to do his homework or practice his instrument. He was putting pressure on himself to excel all the time. But he realized that when he did go with his friends, he had fun, felt better, and could still manage to get his homework or practising done. When he stopped to examine it, he realized that socializing was valuable to him.

It also mattered to him which friends he chose. Examining his relationships, he realized that there were some friends he was happy to spend time with, even if it meant reordering his schedule. There were others, however, who maybe weren't the best kids to hang around, because those interactions brought him down or just didn't feel right for him. He was learning how to make choices for himself that worked in his best interests. This is important, especially in junior high and high school, when kids are around their peers more than they are around their parents. A lot of important choices have to be made at that point, and most often parents won't know what's at stake. For example, adolescents might be invited to a party where they know there will be drugs and alcohol, and they will have to decide if they want to put themselves in a potentially dangerous and illegal situation.

HAVE THE COURAGE TO SAY NO.

Learning how to say no—and as a parent, *letting* your kid say no and mean it—is another essential skill set they need to cope in the world. As any parent can tell you, this starts around the time that a child turns two. You hear people talk about the terrible twos, but I always think of this phase as the terrific twos. It's when they learn that they're separate from us and that they *can* say no—and good for them! It can be tough for parents because suddenly their "babies" are fighting them on all kinds of things. But comfort yourself with the thought that when they get older, they're going to know how to say no when it's important.

As parents, we may imagine that we want perfectly obedient children who will do everything we tell them to and just follow along. But that's the last thing you want because then they're going to blindly follow along with their peers, and that's not a good thing. If kids are constantly expected to "do as they're told," they will. This may include doing what their peers or adults in authority (like coaches or teachers) tell them. This can set them up to be abused or treated poorly.

KIDS FEEL THE PRESSURE.

Kids react to the external pressure to do well at school or in their activities by making it their total focus. The pressure to perform doesn't always come from parents, though. Kids can be perfectionists themselves and can become obsessive high achievers. They can lose a sense of perspective and balance in their lives; they're not getting out and having fun, and that can be draining. They often end up feeling depressed and wondering, *Is this all there is to life—work, work, work?* They need to be encouraged to get out and do more socially and to make their own choices about what kind of nonschool activities and friends they find the most fulfilling.

That ability to say yes and no appropriately will come in handy when your kids become adults. As a society we're awfully busy, and it's too easy to let ourselves be talked into taking on extra jobs or volunteer work, leaving no time for ourselves. Yes, it's nice to be asked, but if we're so busy giving our energy and time to everyone else that there's nothing left for us, that's not healthy either. Learning how to make those kinds of choices begins early in life.

BUILDING CONFIDENCE IN MAKING CHOICES IS LIKE TRAINING A MUSCLE SET.

And regular workouts yield the best results. Don't choose your kid's clothes, food, or friends. Believe it or not, your kid knows what he wants to wear. That also starts at about age two. When my son was that age, he chose his own outfits—and yes, some of them made me cringe just a little. I remember before I was a parent, I used to look at some kids and they'd be dressed in odd, mismatched outfits, and I'd think, *What's wrong with that mother?* Then I had my own and I totally got it. I remember my son marching around in shorts and cowboy boots—his favourite look. He wanted to be a superhero, so he usually wore a cape (or a towel, if his cape was in the wash) and left for school. The other kids were all wearing their perfectly matched little outfits, but he liked what he liked, and that was that. At his first Christmas concert in kindergarten, all of the kids were supposed to wear black pants, but he wore bright green ones. It didn't really matter to me, and everybody thought he was cute. He's always been able to say no to people, so when he hit the age where his peers were into partying and drugs, he had no problem saying no to all of it. He's been given the freedom to make choices that are right for him and allowed to say no to the things that weren't—and that's made all the difference.

HELP YOUR KID TURN UP THE VOLUME ON HIS OR HER INNER VOICE.

Encourage and empower your children to listen to the voice within— the authentic voice of who they are. Teach your kids to tune in to their intuition, their inner-guidance system. One way I help my clients learn to listen to themselves is with a little meditation. I get kids to close their eyes and take some deep breaths, and then I have them imagine a ball of light above them. They choose the colour— whatever feels right to them—and I guide them to feel that colour move down through their body as they imagine themselves going to their "special place." It could be at the top of a mountain or on a beach, or even in an imaginary land of candy and ice cream. Then I ask them if there's someone else there with them—someone they can talk to and ask questions of.

One young client had a problem with sweets. She liked more candy than was good for her, and it was contributing to health and weight issues. She asked her inner self for help making better decisions around her cravings. "Okay," she said. "What is healthy for my body and what should I be doing?" Using this technique helped her tune in to ask herself questions like, "What does my body need right now? Does it need candy right now, or does it need something else?" The choice then became hers: "No, I need some fruit."

Her parents had struggled with getting her to make those kinds of choices more thoughtfully and had finally resorted to taking the options out of her hands. But if you, the parent, are the one saying, "You're not allowed candy," then your child is not learning to regulate herself. Add to that the fact that any time you tell someone they can't have something, they're going to want it all the more. But if you put the choice back in the child's hands, you're empowering her to listen to her own best instincts.

The same goes for how you offer kids food at meal times—there should be a selection of healthy options and no "clean-plate-club" rules. Obviously ice cream isn't going to be an option next to the carrots, but that said, sometimes it's fun to break the rules and have a backwards dinner, starting with dessert first. Not only does it create a fun break from the norm (and a special memory) it also takes dessert out of the "forbidden-fruit" category. If your kids are resentful ("We never get dessert. We never get candy."), they're probably going to go off and sneak it anyway. You'll pack a healthy lunch for them, but they'll go to school and trade their lunch with somebody else. Why? Because it's a battle for control, and they know instinctively that they need to own their choices. When we push too hard to run our kids' lives, they're going to be goaded into running the opposite direction even if that little inner voice is telling them it's the wrong way to go.

Our bodies give us all kinds of cues about the choices we're making, if we're tuned into them. One of my clients, a thirteen-year-old boy, used a method I teach to key into the sensations that were "telling" him what choices to make. I had him close his eyes, take three deep breaths, and then had him scan his body slowly from head to toe. Then I would have him visualize different scenarios and scan his body again. Using a scenario that he already knew was not in his best interest, he felt a tightness in his shoulder and his lower leg. Then, he was able to test other scenarios. He learned that when something wasn't right for him, he felt that same tightness in his shoulder and his leg, and being aware of that helped him to make choices that were right for him going forward.

All of us have these kinds of inner monitoring systems. Sometimes they'll feel like butterflies in our stomach, telling us, "That's not right." There are positive feelings when we're going in the right direction, too; kids discover that when they're saying something that's the right decision for them, they'll literally get goose bumps— or "truth bumps," as I sometimes call them. That's when I say, "Okay. That feels right for you. Those are the friends that you want to be with." Similarly, if they're thinking about sneaking off with other kids, they can tell that it doesn't feel right.

NOT EVERY QUESTION NEEDS A LOGICAL ANSWER.

And not every feeling can or should be explained. Sometimes parents will ask their child, "Why do you want to do that?" Kids really struggle with that kind of question; the "why" puts them on the defensive, when sometimes it's just a feeling or a "knowing." The ability to access intuition can help guide us in the right direction. Everyone experiences intuition a little differently, but it's always there if we listen closely enough. Some of the kids I work with can close their eyes and see a scenario playing out before them like a movie, telling them which way to go. It's important to understand and teach our children the importance of "following their gut" when it comes to making important decisions.

GOOD STUFF HAPPENS WHEN IT'S QUIET.

Occasionally a parent says to me, "My kids says he's bored," and I have to explain that that's sometimes a very good thing. That quiet "bored" time can help kids cut through the clutter of noisy thoughts and find inspiration. During quiet time, kids will get ideas, whether it's about a creative way to tackle a big project or how best to deal with a personal issue. It also gives them a chance to experience and react to the signals their bodies give them as to whether or not what they're doing is the right thing.

I work with kids in these ways, giving them strategies to create more self-confidence, and with their parents, outlining ways they can support, rather than undermine, that confidence. Nothing is more important than that confidence to their future success or their current happiness—and without the opportunity to make choices independently, they can't possibly achieve it.

CHAPTER TWO

TAKING OWNERSHIP— AND RESPONSIBILITY

We all want to raise responsible adults who can make their own decisions and move confidently throughout the world. But too many of us don't know when to relinquish the reins to our kids. There's no magic formula for this; the training wheels have to come off, and sooner is better than later. And there's no time like the present to start giving your child some ownership and responsibility for his or her actions.

I talked a little in the previous chapter about helicopter parenting and the toll it's taking on our kids and young adults. What's driving this trend? Very few of us in my generation had to cope with everpresent parental pressures. When did we become so fretful and controlling?

WHEN DID WE START TAKING OVER OUR KIDS' LIVES?

The rise of helicopter parenting has been a gradual thing, and I'd say much of it is media driven; there's a lot of fear out there about kids being kidnapped or hurt. It used to be that kids could go out and play until the streetlights came on, signalling that it was time to go home. But now, usually both parents are working, and every moment of the day is structured. They're not just going out on the street and playing street hockey anymore; it's Mom or Dad saying, "I'll sign you up for hockey." The adults are driving the activities, which no longer belong to the kids. If your kid isn't in hockey or soccer or dance or whatever's popular, he's effectively socially cut off because his friends are all doing it. I hear families talking about how it's a long weekend or spring break and they're not going on a vacation because their kids are in a hockey tournament. We're forgetting what's important, in my opinion. But if I sit and ask parents, "What is important to you?" they'll usually say, "Family time." Okay—but where is it? When you're dashing here and there to take your kid to some activity or rushing through homework, where is the time to just sit down and have a meal or go outside and lie on the grass and look at the clouds?

We want them to do well in school, so we're all over it: "What's your homework today? When's your project due? Why don't you do it this way?" We think we're helping, but in fact we're hurting our kids, because we want them to become independent, successful adults. But when they've always been told when it's time to tidy their room, put their dishes away, do their homework, and brush their teeth, it's not surprising that they have no clue what to do when they get out on their own—they're so used to being told.

TRY IT: BUILDING ROUTINE

Help your child break it down. Make a list of the steps that need to happen. Then, together, brainstorm ways to get each step done.

Example:

MORNING ROUTINE

- wake up
- brush teeth
- get dressed
- eat breakfast
- pack lunch
- go to school

Let go of perfectionism. If your young child suggests sleeping in their clothes to reduce the steps in the morning, give it a try. Most children's clothes don't wrinkle anyway. Maybe packing lunch or their backpack the night before would help. For teens who have difficulty getting up in the morning, maybe they can set their alarm on the opposite side of their bedroom from their bed. Don't be afraid to be creative. Try it out for a few days, then reevaluate and remember to focus on the successes! Change takes time . . . it won't happen overnight.

The weekday morning routine is a common battleground of family life, one that can be upsetting and disruptive to everyone in the home. One mother came to see me about her nine-year-old daughter because every morning was an ongoing struggle to get her out of the house in time for the bus—getting her to brush her teeth, comb her hair, get dressed, and even flush the toilet was an issue.

I sat down with the girl and said, "First of all, do you like your mom nagging at you to get ready for school?" When she admitted she didn't, I asked her if she'd like to change things, and she agreed that she would. "Okay. Let's start with brushing your teeth. Whose teeth are they?"

"Mine," she answered.

"Okay. So, if you don't brush your teeth, what's going to happen?"

She looked at me in surprise. "They'll rot and fall out."

"Okay," I said, "Is that what you want?"

"No!"

"So what do you need to do?"

"Well, brush my teeth."

We went on from there, working out the details of how she'd get things done in a timely way. She drew up a chart that listed the morning tasks she had to conquer, with strategies to make them easier. For instance, her long, thick hair was always in a painful tangle when she got up, but if she took the time to braid it at night, she realized that problem could be eliminated—and another morning battle along with it.

Afterwards, I talked again with her mother and encouraged her to focus on her daughter's successes. All of her daughter's strategies would require some time and practice to perfect, but it was important to acknowledge and applaud her efforts from the beginning: "Wow, it's great that we weren't fighting this morning."

Within a week, the girl was doing everything on her own, and the morning battles had stopped. She'd taken ownership of the job of getting ready. Not only was there less conflict between her and her mother, but her parents were getting along better with each other, and she was getting along better with her siblings, too, thanks to the tension levels being ratcheted down.

WIN THE SCHOOLWORK WARS.

Schoolwork and homework can be another area of conflict for families. There are all kinds of reasons why kids put off work or don't do what they're supposed to, but as parents, too often we ascribe it to laziness without looking at underlying factors that might be causing the problems. First of all, the concept of a timetable in which work must be completed isn't something that kids innately understand, so they're more likely to procrastinate. Sometimes the problem is with the school itself; maybe that local school isn't the best place for them. It could be that the teaching style of their teacher doesn't match up with their learning style. Or it could be something else going on in the classroom that you're not aware of.

I had one client who was having a hard time getting her classwork done, but it turned out that she was sitting beside someone that was constantly distracting her. When her parents requested that she be moved to a different desk, lo and behold, she started getting her work done at school.

If you become aware that your child is not getting her work done in class, try talking to her about her ideas of what the problem might be instead of falling back on nagging or suggesting that she's lazy or doesn't care about her schoolwork.

We're focused on the homework, but maybe they were made fun of that day and weren't able to focus and get their work done, or maybe they're afraid to go back to school because someone's bullying them. I hear that a lot; parents come in with situations where kids don't want to go to school and are struggling with doing their homework, and the problem turns out to be that there's something disruptive going on at school.

TEACHER TIP: VISUALIZING SUCCESS

Having students visualize themselves being successful, whether it be at understanding concepts, passing exams, or giving a performance, can make a big difference in their success. To show your students how powerful visualization is, have them stand with their right arm up (parallel to the floor). Ask them to turn at their waist, as far to the left as they can go, and to notice how far they are able to twist. Then have them return to standing with their arms down. Next, have them close their eyes and visualize themselves doing this same exercise, only being able to twist even further. Now, have them open their eyes and repeat the exercise. They will be amazed at how this time they are able to twist even further than the first time. Helping kids believe in themselves is one of the best ways to improve their performance and behaviour at school.

Kids struggling with their work are sometimes afraid to approach their teacher for help or to put their hand up with a question in class because they don't want to look stupid and risk being made fun of. Your best course is to help them to strategize: How can they get help another way or at another time? Let them come up with ideas and use their initiative to solve the problem whenever possible.

DON'T DO THEIR WORK FOR THEM.

As parents, we can easily fall into the habit of doing too much of kids' work for them. Sometimes they're working on a big project, and we want to help, but instead of helping, we push them toward doing it our way, without really meaning to. Kids can become too used to you doing the bulk of their work and thinking for them, and they will find ways to keep you doing it. The most damaging aspect of this is that if we are stepping in to help with the homework all the time, the message that we're giving to the kids is, "You're not capable, you can't handle this." We have to support them and their efforts—stepping in and doing it for them or coming up with all the ideas is not helpful in the long run.

STUCK FOR INSPIRATION? TRY MIND MAPPING.

The next time your child asks you for help in coming up with ideas, whether it's for a school project or for solving a personal problem, try teaching them this useful, easy technique.

Sit your child down with a piece of paper and, at the centre, have him write the issue or challenge in a circle. Let's say the project requires the student to create something educational about pets. Draw a line radiating out from the centre, and at its end write a potential solution; for instance, he could design a poster. From that idea, other ideas and needs come up and get their own lines. He might need pictures of animals for the poster or some quotes about pet ownership. Drawing some lines that end in blanks actually stimulates the subconscious; kids' minds will continue solving a problem while they do other things, and the solution will come to them "out of the blue." The same process can be used in place of a standard outline form to draw out ideas for an essay or short story. In teaching my clients how to use this technique, I've found that many of them like to use colours in drawing their mind maps. It's a real spur to creativity.

TIME-MANAGEMENT SKILLS DON'T COME NATURALLY.

The ability to do long-term planning is a skill our kids have to be taught, but they don't necessarily learn it in school. This is especially true when they're younger because they're told what they need to be doing every step of the way. As they get into junior high or high school, their teachers aren't holding their hands anymore, and when they're assigned a big project that's due in a month, they're

Mind map.

supposed to figure out how to plan and get that accomplished. Too often that results in the kids pulling all-nighters because they've failed to do the work incrementally over the allotted time.

How do we teach our kids to schedule their work? Again, the best way is to start with a question that leads them to think it through. That could be a mind map or simply making a list of each piece of the project in the order that it needs to happen: "How long will this part of the process take you?" Make sure they write those deadlines down in their agenda so that they can plan: "This day I'm going to spend half an hour after school working on the first part of my essay." Do help them to break it down, because without that personal accountability and understanding of the scheduling required, they'll never learn to tackle complex, long-term projects.

One of my clients, a girl of about seven, was a student in a weekend Japanese language school. There was significant homework, including a booklet of worksheets. She was responsible for completing ten pages of this per week but hadn't gotten the hang of scheduling it and was falling behind. She and I sat down to discuss strategies; should she do a page and a half a night? Or was there a better way? Ultimately, she decided she'd complete the weekly assignment in two five-page chunks on Tuesdays and Thursdays, which were free of other activities, and put that into her agenda. Her mother had been keeping the worksheet booklet for her, and the girl decided she'd rather keep it in her room and make it her responsibility, so she'd always be able to find it. Letting her make the choice and take the responsibility solved the problem.

Breaking the nagging cycle is good for everyone. As a parent, handing the responsibility of scheduling chores and schoolwork back to your children frees you up to do other things and releases you from having to nag, manage, and schedule on their behalf. Suddenly, you have time to catch up with your partner, do your own chores, or simply relax, and the stress level in your household is dramatically reduced.

"CLEAN YOUR ROOM!"

How many family fights have started with that demand? The mother of a young client came to me at her wits' end. With three sons at home, she felt like all she did was pick up after them. My client was a big Lego fan, but he'd leave them scattered across the floor when he was done playing with them—his mother was tired of it, so she confiscated them. He and I sat down together to talk about how he could solve that problem and get his beloved Legos back. We talked through his building process, and he explained that when he was looking for a particular piece, he'd dump the whole bucket of pieces onto the floor. Now, thinking it through, he decided that it would be easier to pick up after his play if he just rooted through the bin rather than dumping it. Another part of the problem, he said, was that his little brother was always getting into his stuff and scattering it on the floor, and his mother blamed the older brother when she had to clean it up. With some more thought, he hit on the idea of putting those toys up on a higher shelf where his brother couldn't get to them—problem solved.

The messy-room issue was also a big problem for a twelve-year-old client and his mother. His feeling was that since it was his room, it was none of her business. But when we talked about it, he admitted that he didn't really like his room when it was a mess and that it made him uncomfortable to have to pick his way through the clutter. At my prompting, he began to consider which of his stuff he really liked and wanted to keep and what he could get rid of. Making those choices for himself allowed him to keep his sense of ownership. But he had to go through the messy phase to come to that revelation.

Don't be too quick to challenge your children about their messy rooms; remember how important that sense of private space is to them, and give them a chance to experience what messiness feels like. I'm not suggesting you let it turn into a health hazard, but sometimes we have to let them have the time and space to figure things out. Are you picking the dirty clothes up off their floor and putting them into the laundry? If so, you're sparing them the consequences of their choices and perpetuating the problem. What's the worst that could happen if you let the laundry pile up? They might wake up one school morning and discover they have nothing clean to wear. That's when you can say, "Your clothes weren't in the laundry bin, so they didn't get washed." They'll figure out very quickly how to avoid that in the future, or they can learn to do their own laundry. This way you've avoided the argument, and they've experienced the consequence of their choice in a way that will lead them to make better ones.

OWNERSHIP MATTERS.

One mother and her daughter, a nine-year-old client of mine, were constantly fighting the battle of room cleaning. No matter what the mom tried, she couldn't get her daughter interested in taking care of her own space. A conversation between us uncovered the reason why: The girl's mother had decorated the room for her daughter without asking her for her input, right down to the throw pillows (which her daughter hated). The girl had no sense of ownership for what was supposed to be "her" room, and so she had no investment in keeping it tidy. Once the mother understood the source of her daughter's resentment and indifference, the two of them were able to come to an agreement that included getting rid of those throw pillows and handing the ownership and responsibility for the room back to her daughter, where it belonged.

WHEN ARE THEY READY TO LEARN?

I'm often asked at what age children should be tasked with specific chores. I don't think there are any hard-and-fast rules about age-appropriate work, except where safety is concerned. But again, the point is to start them off small and early. Even a very young child can break an egg for you when you're baking together. If it falls on the floor, it's not a disaster—that's a good lesson in and of itself and teaches the child to clean up after him or herself.

Parents know their own children and are the best judges of when they can learn, for instance, to do their own laundry. Start them out with "baby steps." Let the child learn to measure the detergent, sort the clothes, and put them in the washing machine under your supervision a few times, and they'll be doing it independently very quickly. Children are naturally curious and eager to learn new things. Let go of perfectionism; if they do the dusting and miss a few spots, so what? It may take a little longer at first to do your chore with their "help," but it will pay off in more independence for both of you.

THE PAYOFF GOES BEYOND LEARNING SIMPLE SURVIVAL SKILLS.

What does being an active, involved, and contributing member of the family give to your children? More than anything, it provides them with a strong sense of their own self-worth. It shows them that they're capable and that their work matters. It says, "You're important to this family." With that in mind, think about how you address their contribution. Instead of leading off with, "Here's the list of chores you need to do," try, "These are the things that the family needs to get done, so how can we all work together?" Chores can be sorted by preference; if one family member hates unloading the dishwasher but doesn't mind vacuuming, for instance, assign the workload accordingly. Sitting down as a family with a list of weekly or daily chores is a way to sort it all out and come to a consensus. Again, you're all part of a team, working together to get things done, and everyone's contribution matters.

TRY IT: TACKLING CHORES AS A FAMILY

1.   Explain to your kids that they are part of your family and that families need to work together as well as play together.

2.   Allow everyone to brainstorm a list of chores. Be open. Write down their ideas and yours.

3.   Allow everyone to choose which chores they'd like to help with. If one of your children likes to cook, maybe he can make dinner one to two times a week. Maybe he hates dusting but doesn't mind vacuuming. Let him vacuum.

4.   Brainstorm ways to make sure important chores are completed each week. Be open to their suggestions. When they are part of the plan, they are much more likely to follow through.

If your kids are not buying into the idea of working together as a family, you have choices. Rather than getting angry, you can choose to do the chores yourself and let your children know that you will not have time to do things for them, such as packing their lunch, driving them to a friend's house, doing their laundry, and so on. Then, don't do the extra things. Don't get into a battle; just state your position and walk away. After missing a play date or a hockey practice, they may decide that it is worth helping out with chores.

WHAT WORKS FOR YOUR CHILD?

A perfectionist parent can be a difficult taskmaster and too often will fall into the habit of doing things for the child just to make sure that whatever it is gets "done right." For instance, I worked with one mother whose eleven-year-old son depended on her to put his homework in his binder and into his backpack every morning. When I asked her why she was doing something that should have been her son's responsibility, she explained that he was always so rushed in the morning that he sometimes forget to pack everything and wound up at school without all of his homework. Her son and I discussed the issue, and he came up with a simple solution: he'd pack the homework the night before, as soon as it was finished.

LET GO OF THE SMALL STUFF, AND KEEP THE BIG PICTURE IN MIND.

You want to have harmony in your home, yet you're getting upset because your kid hangs his coat on a coat hook rather than putting it on a hanger in the front hall closet. Whose problem is that, really? If what you want is to spend time enjoying your family—not bickering with them—part of the responsibility is yours, as parents, to know when to relax and let go of standards that may not comport with your child's.

Remember, too, how much your child wants to please you, even if that doesn't always seem to be the case. That may affect his or her decision making in a way that isn't necessarily positive. My family moved this past summer, which meant my eleventh-grade daughter had to choose between her old school and the new neighbourhood school. We discussed which she should choose, and I suggested,

"You're the one going to school, so which one will feel better for you? Let's look at the pros and cons."

Either one would've been okay as far as I was concerned. But I noticed that when I presented the "pros" of one school, she'd try to guess whether I was actually pushing her to choose that one over the other. She's very much a people pleaser, and I had to convince her that my only wish was for her to make a choice she was happy with. Yes, I could have chosen for her, based on my criteria, but the fact is that as an adult, she'll be making all kinds of important and complex choices, and practice in this area now will make it easier for her down the line.

Very few choices we make are absolute, but kids are apt to see them that way. If your child is considering playing a sport but is afraid he won't like it, point out to him that it's not a forever decision. If he doesn't care for it, there's no reason he'll have to stick with it, and that's true of many of the choices we make in life.

Sometimes the decisions our kids make may not feel optimal to us; sometimes the work they do may not measure up to our standards, or their rejection of our ideas or contributions can seem like rejections of us. Take a big step back and remember, if your child is thinking independently and making up her own mind about things and how to tackle problems, you're doing a great job—even if she doesn't care for your taste in throw pillows!

CHAPTER THREE

LISTENING ACTIVELY AND HOLISTICALLY

As parents, it's natural that we want to make everything smooth for our kids. Sometimes that manifests itself as stepping in verbally to instruct, contradict, and redirect their thinking when they tell us something negative. But it's much more important to simply listen and not judge. That's harder than it sounds: when your daughter says, "I'm so fat," the knee-jerk reaction is to tell her that she isn't, because we don't like to hear our kids tear themselves down.

A more useful response would be to acknowledge what your kids say and respond regarding what you hear beneath the surface: "Sounds like you're not feeling very good about yourself." Once they know you've really heard what they're saying, that in itself is a relief. Think about it: Let's say you spilled your coffee in your lap on the way to work this morning, and you told a friend about it when you got there. Which would you rather hear? "At least you didn't burn yourself," or "Oh, that's awful! What a rough start to your day." Which would make you feel as though your feelings were being acknowledged? The gift of being heard means that you can move on and turn it around: "Yeah, it was a pain, but I can sponge it off." But if people don't listen to us, then we'll keep trying to be heard, and we get mired in that negativity.

Another thing I see parents do is to try and banish anything negative: "Wipe that frown off your face. You're supposed to smile," simply shuts kids down. Chances are they won't come and talk to us when they have something more serious going on, because they're used to not being listened to. I see this very often in my practice; children just stop sharing important things with their parents because the message they've gotten is that negative information isn't welcome.

An example is a nine-year-old girl who was struggling in school; her mother came to see me, upset because her bright daughter couldn't keep up with her reading and didn't seem to care that she was slipping behind. She was finding reasons not to go to school and was almost always late. When the girl came to see me, she opened up about what the real problem was: she was being bullied, and kids were making fun of her. I helped her to share that with her mom. Together they went to the school and got things sorted out, and everything turned around. It was no longer a struggle to get her to school. I've seen that with a few kids; they don't want to go to school, and when asked why they say, "I don't like my teacher," but when you give them a chance to open up, they will share the real reasons with you. Very often it's a bullying issue they're embarrassed to admit to.

TEACHER TIP:
ENCOURAGING KINDNESS

- Encourage random acts of kindness by having students work together to do something nice for some seniors. It helps kids feel good about themselves when they are doing something nice for other people.

- Facilitate discussions about perspective and judgment. Teachers could show kids what it's like to be judged by having, for example, all the kids with blonde hair have to sit at the back of the classroom for the day. The next day it could be all the kids with brown hair. Then there could be a discussion about what it was like to be discriminated because of hair colour. How did it make them feel?

BE OPEN TO HEARING THE WHOLE STORY.

If your child comes home from school and tells you that someone laughed at her, don't just suggest she shrug it off and move on. Ask her to tell you about it, and listen to what she says. Don't give suggestions; just acknowledge her feelings. If you start in with a pep talk, you won't hear the rest of the story, if there's more to tell. Silence is golden in these moments because it emboldens your child to go on talking and telling, and that's what you want. Too often, we're uncomfortable with silence and move quickly to fill in the space with reassuring words. Better to be quiet and listen.

DON'T BE TOO READY TO RIDE TO THEIR RESCUE.

If your child shares something with you, for instance that he is being made fun of at school, as a parent, your first reaction is likely to be outraged and desire to protect him. But if you jump in right away and say, "That makes me so mad, and I'm going to go in and talk to the teacher," you're not giving your child the opportunity to solve it himself or come up with his own strategy. Don't jump to his defence; as long as he knows that you're there to support him if needs be, the chances are good that he'll be able to come up with an idea of how he can handle this bully on his own, perhaps by going to the teacher himself. If you take over for him and solve the problem, he won't learn how to do it for himself and is likely to feel even more powerless. If he is unable to solve the issue on his own, then you can step in as an advocate for your child.

GIVE THEM ROOM TO MESS UP—AND TO FIX IT THEMSELVES.

Even good kids occasionally do the wrong thing, like shoplift a candy bar from the corner store. What do you do when your child comes to you and admits having done something like this? In the heat of the moment, it's hard to see this as a learning experience for your child—but it should be.

Very often the parental reaction is along the lines of, "You're going to march in there, take it back, and apologize." But your first response should be to acknowledge that it took courage for him to come to you and admit his transgression. *Then* put the ball in his court: "What do you think we should do about it?" Obviously, his confession tells you that he's already feeling guilty about what he's done and wants to make it right. And there may be more to the story—maybe it was his friend who shoved it in his backpack, but if you jump in too quickly with a judgmental response, you often won't get the whole story.

By setting your judgment aside and taking the time to listen and understand your children, you are teaching them to communicate and be honest—to hold themselves accountable. Contrarily, immediately revealing harsh judgment to your children's wrongdoings only furthers their reluctance to communicate with you—and may make them revert to lying.

EVERY CHILD HOLDS THE SEED OF GREATNESS.

It's vitally important for kids to be accepted and honoured for who they are. We have to love them unconditionally and expect them to be great because all kids have their own special gifts and ways of doing things that are unique to who they are. It might not be the way that we'd do it, but that doesn't mean we can't appreciate it.

We get what we expect from our children; for better or worse, they will live up or down to our expectations.

We need to separate the behaviour from the child. Just because a child does something that's bad doesn't make him or her a bad kid. If you get a speeding ticket, that doesn't make you a horrible person. Most likely you were distracted and just weren't paying attention.

It's the same with kids. When they make a mistake, parents need to help them to look at the situation and ask, "How can we make it different next time?" while emphasizing, "I still love you, and you're an amazing kid."

All of us hunger for the kind of love that honours who we are and doesn't falter when we fail to live up to our best selves. Treasure what sets your children apart, and let them know that's how you feel. Often, kids don't feel lovable because they're in quandaries or are experiencing new and confusing feelings that make it hard for them to love themselves. Others' judgments on them affect their self-worth—*Will someone laugh at what I'm wearing, or how I talk, or how I throw a ball?* So often it's that fear of judgment that holds us back. You can't control how they experience the judgment of their peers or their teachers, but if they can come home and know that they're loved just the way they are, that makes a big difference.

MAKE TIME TO BE QUIET TOGETHER.

It's important to spend time just sitting with your kids sometimes, letting them know that you're grateful that they're in your life. It doesn't have to be about praising what they do: "You get good marks at school," or "You scored the goal in your hockey game." It's just, "I love you, and I'm so happy that you're here." Don't forget to be grateful that they're yours. Sometimes it's difficult to remember the pure love we felt for contentious teens when they were babies. Keep those baby pictures around, and look at them often to remind yourself that these really are perfect beings whom we've been blessed with.

TRY IT: EXPRESSING GRATEFULNESS

At dinnertime, go around the table and share one reason you are grateful for each other.

Or write a note about why you are grateful for your children and tuck it in with their lunch, put it in their backpack, or set it on their pillow at night.

Examples:

I AM GRATEFUL FOR YOU BECAUSE . . .

- You give the best hugs.
- You have a great sense of humour.
- You have a wonderful laugh.
- You are thoughtful.
- You are kind.
- You love animals.
- You help me see things from a different perspective.
- You have great courage.
- You never give up.
- You are a good thinker and come up with great solutions.

LISTEN TO TEENS.

When kids move into adolescence and start experimenting with new, more adult behaviours, it becomes even more important that we don't allow ourselves to be surprised into making a remark that's going to shut down discussion. The more we listen, the more they'll share. It's more difficult at this age, because the issues they're dealing with are more complex and frankly more frightening: drugs, alcohol, and sex among them. Knowing they can vent about these things to you without worrying that you're going to judge them is key to keeping that openness between you. Expect that they will screw up—and prepare yourself to zip it when it happens. If your children call you because they're drunk at a party and can't get home, go and pick them up without commenting on their bad decision. Believe me, they're already embarrassed (or will be), and lecturing them at that point is likely to shut down communication in the future. Wait until the next day to say, "Let's sit down and talk. Tell me what happened. What was going through your head?" Keep it nonjudgmental and not accusatory. Hear their story without making assumptions because often we don't have the whole story. Let them tell you how they messed up before moving on to, "How do we fix it? What choices are you going to make next time?" and walking them through those options.

Yes, it's tough to keep quiet at times like these. But consider how you'd feel in a similar situation: If you backed into a car, do you really need your spouse telling you, "You should have been more careful"? No, and hearing that is likely to annoy you, as you're only too aware that you made a mistake. With kids the stakes can be very much higher than that.

A child that feels too afraid or too judged to share his story may decide that he's unloved and unlovable.

The guilt from kids' mistakes can lead them to even greater risk taking, to depression, or even to thoughts of suicide. It breaks my heart when I hear kids say that they don't want to be here anymore, that they think that they messed up so badly that they should just end their life. So many kids struggle in emotional isolation because they're afraid to talk to their parents about what's troubling them.

Nothing is worth losing a child over, no matter how bad it is. Think about that when you're listening to their troubles or confessions, and don't let them feel that you're judging them. Otherwise, you might not get that phone call the next time, and your child might take risks that lead to a far greater tragedy than getting drunk at a party.

HAVE "THE TALK" LONG BEFORE THEY NEED IT.

Conversations about sex should begin long before your child hits adolescence. Use the proper names for body parts, and answer children's questions as frankly and with as much detail as you think they can understand. Yes, it can be awkward: I remember my own son at age five sitting in the bathtub chanting, "Erection! Erection!" because he'd learned about it at school that day. It wasn't awkward for him; for kids that age, the whole subject is more like a science class. They don't have that emotional attachment to it or nervousness, so they will just talk, and they will ask questions. You should strive to give them simple, honest answers. There may come a time when your kid tells you that they've had a sexual experience, and if and when that time comes, you're more likely to hear about it if you've established that pattern of openness about these things early on. Again, don't overreact; be glad that they trust you enough to share that.

Even with all the facts we give kids about sex today, it's amazing how much misinformation still circulates. When you become aware that your children or their friends are experimenting with sex, make sure they understand the potential consequences of those choices, and help them explore their thoughts about that in as dispassionate a way as possible. Pose the question, "If you were to get pregnant, how would you handle that?" But make sure to keep the doors of communication open between you, and see that your children know that if and when anything happens—if they need birth control or a trip to the doctor—that you're there for them.

Understand that no matter what you say, they're the ones who will make the choice. You cannot be there to monitor them every minute, much less monitor their friends. The best thing you can do is to listen to them, inform them, and encourage them to make their choices thoughtfully rather than on impulse. This may not reflect the way you were raised, but if that's the case, you need to do your best to shift your response to something more neutral.

If we're really uncomfortable talking about sex, our kids will pick up on it and they won't want to talk to us. If you're feeling a little bit awkward, find a book to help you get past it. Reading a book together could open up the discussion. Some parents need to talk to someone themselves to prepare to answer their kids' questions, and there's nothing wrong with that. It takes courage to ask for help, yet it is so worth it.

SHARE YOUR OWN STORIES AS A WAY TO ELICIT THEIRS.

Don't be afraid to share with your kids stories about mistakes you've made in your life. Our kids often put us on pedestals, imagining that we somehow got through our own youth without making mistakes.

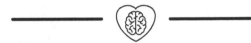

Telling your child about an experience you had or a tough choice you had to make at her age can be a way to show her that it's possible to make a mistake and still grow up to be a responsible adult.

We need to let our kids know that we're human too and we've messed up—and not only in the past. At dinner, I often tell my kids about small stuff like spilling milk on the floor that morning or sending an e-mail to the wrong person. It reinforces their sense that we're all human and we're all fallible—and that that's okay, because we can clean up, apologize, or do whatever it takes to make things right and move on, as long as we're able to acknowledge and take responsibility for our errors.

AVOID ARBITRARY RULEMAKING.

Many of us were raised with inflexible parental rules imposed on us, the reasons for which boiled down to, "Because I said so." We didn't always understand these rules, and many of us broke them on the sly. While I'm not suggesting that all rules are bad, beware of making arbitrary rules without any particular reasoning behind them. Kids understand very well that rules are there because you don't trust them, and the response is often to act irresponsibly, as you've already demonstrated no confidence in their judgment.

Curfews are a good example: Yes, we want to know where our kids are, but it's okay to sit down ahead of a special event they want to go to and negotiate a different time. As long as your kids are clear with you about where they'll be and with whom, there's no reason to be too inflexible. It's also important to understand that sometimes things will come up that may keep them out later than their curfew allows—a problem with a friend, for instance. Instead of countering immediately with a punishment, listen to their explanation first, then tell them to call you the next time they're going to be late. In short, tell them to treat you as they'd want to be treated if the situations were reversed. Haven't you ever come home later than you intended and not because you were doing anything wrong or trying to be sneaky?

If you give kids that opportunity to be open and negotiate, next time they may come home a half an hour early. If you shut them down and impose a punishment, you're encouraging them to be sneakier in the future. If you lay down a hard-and-fast rule about not going to parties, you're pushing your child to tell you that she's going to a sleepover at a friend's house when she's really going to a party. Then, if something goes wrong at the party, she won't call you for help, because she's already lied to you and is afraid of your reaction. Again, the negative consequences can quickly spiral out of proportion to the initial offence.

Don't assume that your child has no judgment or that imposing arbitrary rules will improve that judgment. Judgment is another of those intellectual muscle sets that gets stronger with regular exercise. Give kids the opportunity to develop good instincts and good judgment because you won't always be there to tell them what to do.

A friend of mine did something that I thought was very brave and quite unusual: she told her seventeen-year-old son that she didn't intend to police his actions and that from now on he'd be making his own rules. He'd always been a fairly responsible kid, so she felt safe in being lenient with him. He did very well with this approach and behaved appropriately. Then he went out of town with a school group on an overnight field trip, and someone sneaked liquor from their parents, and the kids got drunk, my friend's son included. The teacher caught them, so when the parents came to pick up their children at the bus, the principal was there to tell them what had happened. Naturally the boy's mother was upset and wondered if she should blame herself. She asked him, "Did I mess up by giving you too much freedom? Is that why you did this?"

He said, "Mom, if you had been stricter, you would have just made me a better liar." On his own, he wrote letters of apology to the teacher and the principal, and he now feels more confident in making wiser decisions.

FOCUS ON THEIR SUCCESSES, NOT THEIR FAILURES.

Keeping your interactions positive is particularly important when our kids are feeling like they've failed us. They do love us, and they want us to love them and to like what they're doing. When they make mistakes, chances are that they're already beating themselves up, so we don't need to add to it. We sometimes presume we know why our kids do (or don't do) certain things, but we often presume incorrectly.

Examples of things that your kids don't want to hear—and that you don't need to say—could include the following:

- "You don't do your homework because you're lazy."

- "You don't help around the house because you don't care."

- "I don't believe you."

- "I can't trust you."

Maybe that homework was too hard for your kid or he just had a fight with his best friend and didn't feel like doing it. Maybe your daughter came in late because of some emotional drama you're unaware of and that she doesn't feel safe sharing with you. There's so much more going on under the surface, especially in adolescence, than we're unaware of as parents—so making judgments based only on what we can see is a bad idea.

Much of our own childrearing has to do with baggage from our own childhood. Maybe we didn't do as well as we should have at school or in our careers, so we push our children to accomplish what we feel we failed at. Or maybe we always wished that we could have played a sport or a musical instrument—and we didn't get the opportunity to, so we're going to live through our kids. That's not fair to them.

GRATITUDE IS AN ATTITUDE.

Model positivity: focus on success— both yours and others'.

We all fall into the habit of beating ourselves up for what we don't get done, whether it's life goals or simple, day-to-day things. And the negative attitude that habit spawns transmits itself to those around us, especially our kids. Count up the things you did get done and think about the compliments or reinforcement you got during the day. Talk about those at the dinner table. Encourage your kids to do the same and to share, for instance, the funniest or the best thing that happened that day. Changing the focus to being grateful for all we did get done can flip the switch on our whole experience, and sharing it with those we love shows them how to make the most of each day.

I often talk about gratitude with my clients: "What are you grateful for? What did you do today? Did somebody give you a compliment today, or did you do well on an exam?" Sure, there might be some things in their day that weren't so great, but if we focus on what went well, we can build on that instead of on the negative. If your kid made his bed this morning, don't fret because the corners weren't perfectly mitred, because if you do, you're robbing him of the accomplishment and the initiative to repeat it.

TRY IT: EVEN MORE GRATEFULNESS

- Have family members write out what they are grateful for on small pieces of paper. Put them in a jar. At the end of each week, read them out loud together.

- At the dinner table, have each person share the best thing about his or her day.

CHAPTER FOUR

TEACHING KIDS TO HONOUR THEIR FEELINGS

Feelings can be frightening to kids as well as their parents. When kids have powerful emotions like anger or frustration, it can be overwhelming for them to know what to do with those emotions. It's hard to sit with your children when they're sobbing, but it's important to honour their feelings and to let them express them because the more we tell them, "Oh, you're okay," or encourage them to sweep their feelings under the rug, the more they'll be inclined to deny and repress them. Powerful emotions don't just disappear when we push them down; they pop up in other ways, like sleep problems or illness. The beautiful thing is that when you allow yourself or your child to feel those emotions, they pass through quite quickly. It doesn't have to be a long, drawn-out thing.

It's when we tell others or ourselves, "You're okay, don't cry," that we're risking worse trouble. As a child, I suffered from emotion-related asthma. My dad flew helicopters and would be gone for weeks at a time, and I got sick every time he went away. When he'd call my mother to pick him up at the airport, my symptoms would disappear almost immediately.

Anger can be frightening in its expression, both to onlookers and to the person who's angry, so many of us repress it. Girls in particular have a hard time expressing their anger, largely because society tells us it's somehow not "ladylike." But anger can be a great motivator: it makes us want to change things rather than putting up with the same old stuff.

HELP YOUR KIDS ACKNOWLEDGE AND OWN THEIR FEELINGS WHEN THEY'RE YOUNG.

When your kids cry over something, even if it's as small as being told no when they ask for a toy at the store, say, "You're feeling sad because you can't have that today." Help them to recognize and name their feelings. It's far better to acknowledge, "Oh, you skinned your knee. That really hurts," and let them cry. Then they will move through it quickly, and they'll also know, *This is what it feels like when I'm sad (or hurt or mad or frustrated).* Show them different ways in which they can calm themselves. One of the things that I teach kids is the simple gesture of putting their hand over their heart and taking a few deep breaths when their feelings are overwhelming them. This helps to bring their attention within, and it's a great way to self-soothe. Parents can hug their kids "heart to heart," or with younger children, can gently rock them.

Share your own feelings with your child, too. Children are great at picking up on our feelings; even when we want to pretend that everything's okay, they know when something's off. They don't necessarily know that Mom's having a bad day or Dad's worried about something, but they'll pick up on your feelings and reflect that stress by acting out or being cranky.

Many of our concerns are adult matters: concerns about finances or getting bad news about a friend's health, for instance, are things we might not want to share with our kids. Even so, you can tell them that you're feeling sad or having an off day. Let them know what you plan to do for yourself to help deal with that feeling: "I'm going to talk to Daddy later," or "I'm going to take a nice bubble bath." That way they can see that even though Mom's not having a great day, she has a plan for handling it. That takes the pressure off of them and helps them understand why they may be feeling off-kilter. Again, never underestimate kids' ability to tune into what you and others are feeling. My own children know me so well that they can tell if I'm stressed just by the tone of my voice or my body language, even if I'm not talking about what's bothering me.

Highly empathic children are affected by everything going on around them, including tensions in their classrooms. If the children around them are angry or sad, they can become overwhelmed by the stress of those feelings and sometimes need help in guarding against that. When I work with children like this, they've often been brought to me because they're resisting going to school. Sometimes they're sad, and they don't understand why until we talk it through and discover that their best friend was sad that day, and they were picking up on it. When I work with kids like this, I teach them to visualize themselves safe inside of a rainbow bubble. They can see what's happening, but the bad feelings can't get through to them.

TRY IT: VISUALIZING A SAFE SPACE

Have your child stand with her feet flat on the floor. Have her imagine tree roots growing out of the bottom of her feet, down through the floor and into the earth. Give her a minute or so to "feel" the tree roots growing down. Then have her imagine herself in a magic bubble. It can be rainbow coloured, her favourite colour, or whatever colour first pops into her mind. This sets an intention of being protected and helps block out negativity from others. When she is ready she can open her eyes. I recommend doing this on a daily basis.

TEACH YOUR KIDS TO SEE AND READ OTHERS' EMOTIONS.

Children need to be able to spot what others are feeling, and it's a simple thing to help them to learn. When you're reading a book together, it's fun to look for and name the expressions on characters' faces; encourage the child to identify the feelings the character is expressing, whether it's sadness, anger, joy, or surprise. You can do the same thing when you're watching a movie together or when you're out and about. Helping your child to understand the visual cues to others' feelings will make your child more empathic and understanding of others and better able to navigate in the world.

TRY IT: RECOGNIZING EMOTIONS

- With young children: Next time you're reading a book together or watching a movie, make a game of identifying emotions the characters are feeling. There are many apps to help kids learn to identify emotions.

- With older kids: Play a game of guessing someone else's emotions just by looking in their eyes, or have an "emotion of the week" and discuss that emotion and ways to handle it.

WHAT HAPPENS WHEN YOU DON'T SHARE YOUR FEELINGS?

When we shield our children from the negative things going on in our own lives, we might imagine we're doing them a favour. But often, we're creating greater anxiety for them. Let's say you've had an argument with your spouse in the morning, but you don't say anything to the kids. Even so, they will pick up that there's something wrong between Mom and Dad and may start to worry that the problem is bigger than it is—*Oh, Mom and Dad are going to get a divorce*—when in fact it was just a little disagreement, and in the evening everything's fine again. Your kids could be worried about that all day long, even blaming themselves if they get a notion that they somehow precipitated it. When you talk to your kids about things like this, you certainly don't need to go into detail. But you can allay a lot of anxiety by simply saying, "Mom and Dad had a little argument, but we've got it worked out. It's okay now." Don't try to pretend that those things don't happen.

When something serious does occur in your lives, you need to acknowledge that. Just make sure your children know that you're dealing with it, that you have a plan of action, and that it's not up to them to solve the problem for you.

ENCOURAGE YOUR CHILD TO CHANNEL FEELINGS IN A SAFE WAY.

Kids in the grip of a strong emotion like anger often feel like they can't safely release it. We only add to that burden when we say things like, "Don't be mad at your brother." The fact is that sometimes brothers do things that make each other mad, and that's okay. A more useful approach is, "Okay, so you're mad. Now what do we do with that? You can stomp your feet. You can go punch a pillow. You can take some clay and squish it." As kids get older they can vent by drawing pictures or writing angry letters and ripping them up rather than internalizing the anger or acting out on someone else. Once they've calmed down, you can help them to talk through the feelings they had and how to deal with the situation that precipitated those feelings.

One common challenge I hear about from my young clients is the frustration of working on group projects at school, when one member gets stuck doing all the work for the others in the group. The person who winds up doing the work rightfully resents having to do so, and it's a chance for me to lead them through the process of choosing (when possible) a more reliable partner the next time around. I also advise them to tell the person they worked with this time that they're not happy with how it went and that they're not going to choose to work with them the next time around. If partners are assigned, then I would encourage them to discuss the issue with their teacher.

WHEN KIDS REPRESS THEIR FEELINGS, THOSE FEELINGS COME OUT IN OTHER WAYS.

A concerned mother brought her seven-year-old daughter to see me; her daughter's daily stomachaches were keeping her home from school, but the doctor couldn't find anything wrong with her. Together, she and I did a meditation exercise. I had her close her eyes and scan her body. I said, "Okay, I want you to talk to your stomach and ask it why it's hurting you all the time."

She said, "I want to spend more time with my mom." She had three siblings, and one was quite young and took up lots of her mom's time.

I said, "Okay, let's figure out a way. Mommy's got lots of things to do. If you would like Mommy to have more time with you, is there something that you could do to help her so that she could have a little bit of extra time?" Some of the ideas she came up with for freeing up time for her mother were unpacking her lunch box and backpack when she got home and making her own lunch for school. She presented those ideas to her mother, who was very touched; the two of them both enjoyed doing crafts, so they made a plan to have regular craft time together every week as special time just for them. With the solution to her problem, her stomachaches disappeared and didn't come back. Headaches and even dizziness can manifest when kids' feelings go unheard. Sore throats often mean that they really have something that they need to say, but they're holding it back.

Anger is another common indicator that feelings are being repressed or going unacknowledged. Who wants to be around a kid who's angry or frustrated? It's not fun, and we often respond by saying something like, "Go to your room and don't come out until I see a smile on your face." But it's important to let them express their anger because otherwise it will come out some other way. One boy I worked with came to me because his parents were fighting with him for a good two hours a night to get him to turn off his computer and video games and go to bed. He'd been an affectionate and easygoing kid, and this new side of him was upsetting to his parents.

It didn't take me too long to discover what the source of his anger really was: as a middle child sandwiched between an older brother and a demanding younger sibling, he craved one-on-one time with his mother. His mom was astonished; after all, she drove him to all of his activities and took care of him. But what he wanted more than anything else was just to hang out with his mom and bake brownies. That sounded reasonable to me, so we discussed ways that he could help his mother out around the house so that she could make time to bake with him. She was in the midst of trying to start a business, so her time was pretty tight. He agreed that he would entertain his younger brother for a couple of hours in the afternoon so that his mom could go in her office and get some work done. Then they set aside time on Saturday to bake brownies together. That was a win-win solution that really underlines how important it is to check in with our kids.

Feelings too big to handle can spark depression, and depression can manifest itself in many different ways—not all of them easily recognizable.

A young, ninth-grade client of mine was struggling with his feelings for a friend who was herself having a hard time with depression. His mother initially called me because he was uncharacteristically angry and had knocked over a desk chair. When we got together, he was slumped in his seat, his posture closed, clearly not eager to talk. I encouraged him to tell me about the things that he liked to do. He started talking about magic tricks, and I could see the positive shift in his attitude and posture immediately. As it happened, I had a deck of cards handy, and I asked him to show me a trick. He gladly complied, and I could see his delight in my amazement at his skill.

I said, "Every day I want you to take some time to do some magic for somebody." It was clear that this nurtured him and made him feel good. Even if it was just five or ten minutes' worth, it was a great treat for him and for the person he shared it with, and it reminded him of what made him happy. Parents, if your children have a passion for something, whether it's card tricks or music or writing poetry, encourage them. The good feelings they associate with their hobby will carry over into their feelings about themselves and their worth. It can even help them with things they don't find easy or pleasant.

This includes schoolwork. Many of my clients tell me they "can't do math" or are bad at it. I encourage my young clients to think about something they are good at. We discuss how, when they are good at something, they usually do it over and over because they enjoy it. In other words, they practice. Their capacity to be good at something with practice can be carried over to other things, including math. Also, finding someone to help them in a way that works for them can make a big difference. For example, if they are good at playing soccer, they practice. They may be really good at scoring but need to practice passing the ball. With practice and tips from a coach, they will improve at their passing. With encouragement, some helpful tips, and practice, they can become much better at math skills as well.

TEACH KIDS TO TRUST THEIR FEELINGS.

It is very important that we allow our children to feel and acknowledge their emotions. Very often, in wanting to help make things easier for our kids, we brush off their feelings. For example, if they fall and skin their knee and start to cry, we often say something like "Oh, you're okay. It doesn't hurt." Yet, the truth is, it does hurt. If they are unhappy, some parents will send their kids to their room and tell them they can come out when they have a smile on their face. This teaches kids not to trust their own feelings and to hide them. Our emotions give us so much information. Kids need to be able to trust and honour their own feelings, as they can help kids make wise decisions.

Kids come under a lot of pressure from their peers to feel or think in particular ways. Often their feelings conflict with those norms, and they're confused by it. A ten-year-old girl had been brought to me because she was being bullied at school. We met several times. As we worked through those issues and others, she mentioned that she'd been invited to a party. Something in her tone told me that she was less excited than I'd have expected her to be, and I asked her about that. She admitted that there were kids who'd be at the party who'd been mean to her in the past and scared her. But the expectation was that if you're asked to a party, you go, so she had accepted despite her misgivings.

I reassured her that she could in fact say no if she didn't want to go. I had her close her eyes and say, "Imagine you're going to this party. I want you to scan your body and see what it feels like." When she told me she felt clenching in her abdomen, I explained "That's your body telling you that that's not a good thing for you to do." Then I had her visualize something she enjoys doing—in this case, her volunteer work raising money for the children's hospital—and I asked, "How does that feel in your body?" She reported a pleasurable sense of goose bumps. "Okay, that's what your body shows you if you imagine doing something that's a good thing. When your stomach is clenched up and in knots, your body is telling you that's not a good thing for you to do." Teaching kids to "check in" with their body's responses helps them make good decisions for themselves. The more they practice this kind of internal "listening," the more acute they become at reading and honouring their real feelings.

Teaching kids to "check in" with their body's responses helps them make good decisions for themselves.

JUST . . . LISTEN.

Very often, parents let their own anxieties dictate their responses when they should be letting their children vent without judging. If your high school-aged kid comes to you saying how much he hates a particular class or school in general, your response is likely to be coloured by your anxiety about him doing well enough to get into college. But simply insisting that he has to do well and suck it up is just going to make him shut down. Instead, listen first to what he has to say, and acknowledge it: "Wow, that doesn't sound like a fun class to be in." Let him talk; just listen. What that tells him is that you understand. As we've noted, the issues around kids' dislike of school or a particular class may be about something else entirely—bullying or fear of failure, for instance. But you'll never find out if you let your own anxieties cloud your ability to listen. So many kids today turn to the Internet to vent or to seek out advice on their problems—and that world can be pretty dark and dangerous.

Sometimes when you're trying to talk through feelings with your children, you'll notice that they don't seem to be paying attention. Perhaps they're not making eye contact, or they're fidgeting around with something. Usually this signals some level of discomfort with the intimacy of the feelings they're talking about, and you shouldn't insist on eye contact at times like these. Instead, let them have their space while you're talking with them. It really helps, especially with boys, if they have something else that they can be doing. That's why having conversations in the car is so great, because for one thing, your kids are strapped in and can't get away from you. But also there isn't that eye contact, and that makes it easier for them to be open and honest.

When I'm working with clients, I'll let them play with Lego sets or Play-Doh or let them draw while we talk. You might think they'd be too distracted, but that's often when I get the very best information out of them, because not having to look at me frees them to be more open. Many times I've had kids say, "I haven't told anybody else this," even a teenage boy who was feeling that he was probably bisexual. His parents didn't know, but he was able to tell me. But again, we weren't sitting across from each other looking eye to eye. He was playing with a wire puzzle as we talked, and that gave him the space he needed to tell me what he was thinking.

TRY IT: TOUGH CONVERSATIONS

The next time you're having a tough conversation, allow your children to avoid eye contact. They will be more likely to open up while looking out the window, drawing, or doing something with their hands.

You can use this technique, too; that's why so many fathers and sons report having their most profound conversations with each other when they're outside tossing a baseball back and forth, for instance.

Trusting our feelings includes not only our emotions but also our body sensations. These sensations include things like a knot in our stomach, hair standing up on the back of our neck, or goose bumps. These are all signals our body gives us. Learning to trust these sensations is very valuable. Have you ever noticed how someone can walk into a room in a great mood and you start to feel lighter and happier, or maybe someone is angry and you feel heavy and you begin to feel uncomfortable? You may get an idea for something and then get goose bumps, or truth bumps, as I like to call them. For me, getting goose bumps tells me I am on the right track. It is important to teach kids to trust their feelings not only to help them make decisions but also because doing so can help keep them safe.

We often teach kids, "Don't talk to strangers." A more useful rule would be, when you meet someone, listen to what your body and instincts are telling you. Some people you like right away. Others give you an icky feeling, even though they might be outwardly very pleasant. In both cases, we're picking up on that person's vibration: Everything is energy, including our thoughts and emotions. When we are happy and in joy, the cells in our body vibrate quicker than if we are feeling angry or frustrated, when our cells vibrate slower. Kids are very in tune to that subtle change. If we think about it, we can be too. There are times when we've just met somebody and right away there's that instant connection. That tells us that person is in a good place; they're happy and joyful, and we sense it immediately. But there are also times when we feel, *I don't really want to be around that person,* and we don't know why. It may not make logical sense, and that's okay. If somebody doesn't feel right, go the other way. And please, don't push your kids to hug anyone they're not inclined to hug, even if it's a relative. They need to be able to honour their feelings and their body and be able to say no—and for that to be okay.

HELP YOUR CHILD CREATE A FIRST-AID KIT FOR THEIR FEELINGS.

An exercise I do with my clients is something you can do at home, too. I like to get kids to create personalized first-aid kits for their feelings. They put in pictures of those they love and care about—

their parents, their family, their friends, their pets. They might have a playlist of music that they like, a special little treat like a candy, or if they're older, a packet of tea or something, and a package of Kleenex to remind them that it's okay to cry. A favourite rock or crystal serves as a reminder that they're strong. Play-Doh or a squishy ball is a great way to release anger or tensions for a younger child; an older one might have a journal to write or draw in to express their feelings. Some little thing shaped like a heart—whether it's made of paper, stone, or fabric—is included to remind them that they are loved. This little first-aid kit stays private and in a safe place, perhaps by the bed. When bad feelings bubble up, they can open it and use the contents to remind themselves that they're strong, loved, and will be okay.

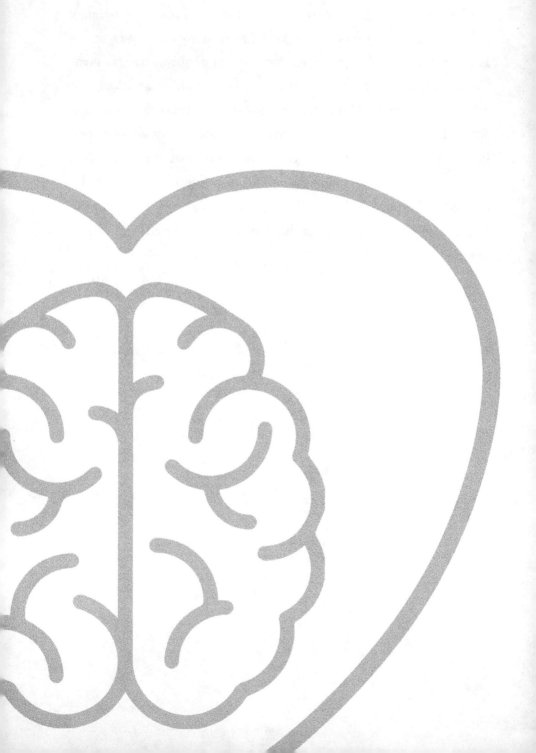

CHAPTER FIVE

MAKING TIME FOR FUN

L ife should be fun. I doubt anyone would disagree with that, yet how many of us actually schedule time for fun? When we take life too seriously, it makes everything harder. We should be able to enjoy special moments together because the time goes by so fast, and memories are what we're left with. So often I've heard older people say they wish they'd spent more time goofing around with their kids when they were little. My kids and I often laugh about good times we had when they were small. But the good things about having fun go beyond making memories and building stronger relationships. When we're having fun and laughing, it boosts our immune system and lowers the levels of stress hormones in our bodies, so it also helps to keep us healthier.

Those happy memories of moments together are what are really important in life. It's not about the house or car we have; it's about those relationships, those special connections and memories. Life can change in an instant. Make sure you don't regret not doing fun things with your kids.

There are ways that we as adults like to spend our leisure time, but I think it's also important to find out from our kids what they enjoy. For example, the parents may love skiing, so family vacation may be spent at a lodge on the slopes. But maybe that's not what their children truly love; maybe they'd like to paint or ride bikes. Sometimes it may not be things that we enjoy (or that we assume we wouldn't), but we can take that time to let the kids share what they love and teach us.

Have you ever noticed how your child lights up when you give him the chance to teach *you* something for a change? As I mentioned previously, many kids around the age of five or six are into dinosaurs; they know how to pronounce their names, what they ate, and where they lived. Other kids are into sports teams or games. Have you asked your child to explain his interest to you and to teach you what he knows? Giving your child the chance to teach you builds his self-confidence and provides you with an opportunity to bond over the activity. When kids are feeling confident and happy and are having fun and laughing, they're able to let go of stress.

TRY IT: LEARN FROM YOUR CHILD

Set aside thirty to sixty minutes on the weekend to give your child the opportunity to teach you or share with you something that he or she loves. Pay attention, and attempt to see things through your child's eyes.

Even when something goes wrong, the attitude with which you approach it can make the difference between an unhappy, stressful interaction and a light-hearted one. If a kid spills the milk, are you more likely to say, "You always do that, and now I've got to clean up the mess," or "Oh well. Isn't that silly?" and then make a game of cleaning it up? When I used to clean up toys with my children, we'd sing songs or make a game of it to see who could clean up their part fastest. They enjoyed it and so did I. Everybody wins when we can have fun. Sometimes if you do something goofy in a stressful situation, it can just turn things around. You may also find that your child's angry, stressed response to what should be a minor irritation is related to a bigger issue lurking under the surface, one she isn't comfortable about bringing up. If you can diffuse the minor irritation with some silliness and get her to laugh, you can often get to what the real issue is and come up with a solution or a way to cope.

When we're having fun with our kids, we're more approachable, too, and they'll come and talk to us. Very often I hear from parents that their teens shut down and don't want to talk to them. Being able to have fun and do something silly together can help to bridge that divide, prompting them to open up and rebuild that connection. And I'm not necessarily talking about going on a vacation or even taking a whole day for fun (although those are great options). It can be something small. Very often I will give bubbles to my clients. It doesn't matter how young or old you are; it's always fun to blow bubbles, and that's a great way to relieve stress. Cooking something together is fun for older kids, as is letting them create a meal on their own. Play board games, or sit with the family photo album and share stories about when they were little. Kids love this. These kinds of things are low cost or free, they're easy, and they don't take much special planning.

While I understand how busy parents are these days, I think that having a date with each of your kids once a week is great. It could be just half an hour, and it doesn't always matter what you do together as long as it's just the two of you. So many kids tell me that they wish they had more time with their parents, and when you carve out special time just for them, it's tremendously meaningful. Again, this doesn't have to be a big effort. It could be going to the library, taking a hike, or going and getting an ice-cream cone. It's the time you spend that matters and lets your kid know that she matters, too.

TRY IT: ONE-ON-ONE TIME

Schedule a date with each of your kids, once a week for at least a half an hour. Focus on letting your children know that they are special to you and that you enjoy spending time together doing things that they find enjoyable.

Here are a few date ideas:

- Young kids: Go outside for a walk and let them explore; collect rocks, leaves, and sticks; or watch bugs. Take a trip to the zoo or the playground. Have a picnic in your living room. Throw a blanket on the floor and invite their stuffed animals to have "tea."

- Older kids: Hike, swim, or snowshoe. Dance around the living room. Bake together, have movie night complete with popcorn, hit the amusement park, or go through a drive-through and buy coffee for the person behind you. Leave happy sticky notes in random places for people to find (and watch their reactions). Do a craft together. Look at baby photos.

Little things do mean a lot; try changing up your routines to bring unexpected fun home. Put on an upbeat song and dance around the kitchen when you're making breakfast. Tuck a loving note into your child's lunch. Do a random act of kindness, encourage your kids to do them, too, and share your stories about them around the dinner table. I encourage kids to write things like "I like your smile," or "Have a great day" on sticky notes and put them in random places for people to find. When kids are doing something for somebody else, it helps them to feel happier and more confident, and it's great to encourage those acts of philanthropy by making them a family activity. Suggest shovelling a neighbour's driveway or bake them some cookies together.

You could invite a friend or two over for a craft project; play dress up and take silly photos with your phone; or rearrange their room (let them provide the ideas). You're really only limited by your imagination, and that time is such a gift for our kids and for us. We may be stressed out in our jobs, but if we can come home and have fun with our family, it makes it less stressful. An added bonus comes when your child becomes a teen: If you've built a relationship in which you have fun together, you'll find that they're less likely to be rebellious or disrespectful and rude to you. They're more likely to be cooperative if you ask them to do something because they've seen that you make time to do things with them.

Be willing to venture out of your comfort zone and try something new with your child. I was awed when a friend of mine recently took her teenaged son skydiving—what a memory for them to share! It doesn't always have to be that extreme, but don't be afraid to try something different. It might be something like taking a dance class together or going to a basketball game, even if sports aren't your thing.

DO YOUR ACTIONS MIRROR YOUR VALUES?

What are your family values? Often, parents will tell me, "It's family time, having time together." Yet they're always busy driving their kids from one activity to the next, especially for kids involved with sports. Those schedules can cut into things like family vacations or together time.

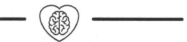

Screen time too often replaces together time. Time together often involves cellphones and other electronics. Make sure to have time without these.

Look around the next time you're at a restaurant and see how many families at tables together are all on their phones, checking e-mails or texting—and I'll bet the parents are doing it too, not just the kids. Put the phones away, folks, and have a conversation with each other. Aren't your kids as important as whoever is e-mailing you? Spend the time talking to each other and making that human connection. Make a "no-screens-at-the-table" rule, and stick to it. It will pay off for all of you in better communication and fewer fights.

Down the line, when your kids are around peers who are using drugs and alcohol, having that connection with you at home means that they're going to be less stressed, more able to resist peer pressure, and less likely to be looking for ways to "check out." If they go home and feel loved, comfortable, and relaxed, they're not going to need to go to the party and get drunk, because they won't need that for an escape. On the other hand, if they're alienated at home, or if their interactions with their parents are confrontational and noisy, that's not a fun place to be, so they're more likely to say, "I'm out of here. I'm going to hang out somewhere else." In the long run, it's a huge benefit to take that time, even though we're busy and have lots on our minds. It's good for us. I know that when I'm having a rough day and thinking, *I've got so much to do*, if I take a little bit of time to goof off and laugh with my daughter, I feel better. It's a great way to change the mood and teaches our kids the coping skills they'll need to be happy, confident, and resilient adults.

FUN CAN DEFUSE A FIGHT BEFORE IT STARTS.

When my son was little, it was next to impossible to get him out of bed on school mornings. Instead of standing at the door and shouting at him, I'd go to his sock drawer and start pitching balled-up socks at him. Once I pulled his sheet off the bed with him on it and dragged him downstairs as he giggled. Some days I'd go in singing "You are my sunshine" and start a pillow fight.

Use fun as a way to encourage and support an attitude of gratitude. In our house we kept a Joy Jar, and at dinnertime the kids would share the good things that had happened or things that they were grateful for that day, write them down on slips of paper, and put them in the jar. On New Year's Eve, we'd dump out the jar and read them aloud.

Get creative with traditions and come up with some new ones as a family. This is a great thing to do with older kids around the dinner table. Ask them, "What traditions would you like to create?" Maybe they'd like to have roast beef instead of turkey this Christmas or to open gifts on Christmas Eve rather than in the morning. Holidays can be stressful, but they ought to be fun, and if you can come up with ideas for ways to amp up the fun, why not change things up? This is especially good if parents are separated or divorced. Make new traditions!

FUN CAN CREATE COMMUNICATION.

A good way to mix fun with communication is via a game, particularly with teens, who are often disinclined to share information about themselves with their parents. One game I've found particularly useful lets players draw a question card and answer it. For example, "What is your favourite thing to talk about when you are with your friends?" or "If you could suggest one solution to end the violence among teenagers, what would it be?" It gets your kids talking to you, and they appreciate the fact that you want to know what they're thinking.

For bedtime, snuggling up and reading together is great. Stargazing is another fun nighttime activity, and there are apps for your phone that can help you to identify constellations. Self-help guru, Wayne Dyer used to say that the last five minutes before you fall asleep are so important because whatever you're thinking about right before you go to sleep goes into your subconscious, and you marinate in it all night long. That's why I give my clients a recording with affirmations and suggest that they listen to it right before they go to sleep, along with a meditation that I create and record for them. It makes a difference because when you're thinking about positive things as you fall asleep, you wake up in the morning thinking, *Today is going to be a great day.*

TRY IT: BEDTIME ROUTINE

Before bed each night, spend time with your children focusing on something positive. This could mean looking at beautiful photos, listening to a meditation, or simply talking about something good that happened that day.

DON'T WAIT UNTIL YOU'RE A GRANDPARENT TO HAVE FUN WITH THE KIDS.

When I hear people talking about their grandchildren and how much fun they have with them, they often add that they didn't take the time to have fun with their own kids. I don't know about you, but I don't want to wait for grandchildren before I have fun; I want to enjoy my kids now. Can you imagine if we were all doing things that we love to do and had more fun together? How would it change the world? Do your part; be the instigator. Your kids will joyfully follow your lead.

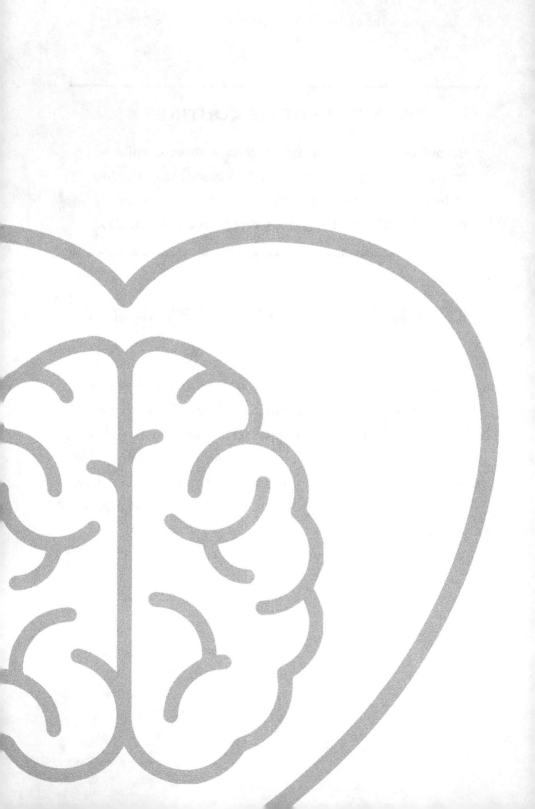

CHAPTER SIX

OWNING YOUR OWN FEELINGS

You may imagine that you can hide your feelings from your kids. You're wrong. Our children know us better than we think, and they're paying attention. They're highly empathic and pick up on our energy. They may not understand everything they're picking up, especially when they're young. Lots of kids have anxiety around leaving Mom, such as when going to school or to play groups, and some of it is just because they are sensing changes in Mom's energy. If they walk into a room and there's been an argument, they feel it, but they don't know why. They just know that something doesn't feel right to them.

If you're having an off day, they feel it. If you try to cover that up and say to them, "No, nothing's wrong, I'm doing fine," they will either worry that whatever it is is so bad that you're afraid to tell them, or they'll start to not trust the feelings that they're getting—

that inner-guidance system that we all have but that we too often just shut off. We've talked about how important it is to teach your kids to listen to and honour that inner voice—important not only for their mental health but also for their safety. But as parents we sometimes fail to model that behaviour ourselves, and unfortunately, the kids get that message.

We often justify these little deceptions by telling ourselves that they're just kids; they can't handle our adult worries. But life throws things at us all, so trying to protect kids by pretending bad things don't happen is just going to hurt them down the line. Do you want your kids to grow up thinking that adults never quarrel, for instance—or worse yet, that their quarrels are so terrifying that they're too awful to acknowledge? Those aren't healthy attitudes for them to internalize, but those are the kinds of conclusions they're likely to draw if you and your spouse quarrel and then pretend everything's fine when the tension is still in the air. It's much better to say, "Mom and Dad had a disagreement. Right now we're mad at each other, but we'll get through it." Parents have arguments with each other; parents also have arguments with kids. If you can argue with respect and understand that sometimes you're not going to agree on things, you can show your kids how to handle those inevitable frictions—that sometimes you need to agree to disagree, or to make a compromise. Those are coping skills they'll need down the line.

If you are having lots of arguments, either with your spouse or your kids, it's important to seek help from a professional. It's very important to model respectful communication and behaviour. This includes using "please," "thank you," and "excuse me" as appropriate in your interactions, speaking calmly, and not disciplining your children in public or in front of their friends. Treat your children the way you want to be treated.

SOMETIMES YOU HAVE TO TALK ABOUT THE REALLY BAD STUFF.

Of course, not every adult problem is as simple as a family quarrel. Let's say the doctors found something suspicious on your mammogram, and you need to go in and have a biopsy. Of course you're worried. How do you share that with your kids when they ask you what is wrong? Your first inclination will probably be to brush it off, but they are going to notice that you're distracted and won't buy it.

Your best bet is to be honest without going into too much detail: "Well, I've got to go for some tests. I'm a little bit concerned about something, but I'm sure everything will be fine. I'll let you know." As a nurse, I know how quickly we automatically start thinking the worst when a health problem comes up: *Oh my gosh, I've got this lump. It's going to be cancer.* That negativity is a knee-jerk response for most of us, but it's something we can address and examine. Am I 100 percent sure it's going to be cancer? Well, no. Am I 100 percent sure it's not going to be? No. Because I can't be sure either way, I'm going to choose to go with the idea that it's going to be nothing.

When you're able to deal with your own anxiety in this way rather than letting it run away with you, you're naturally going to transmit less anxiety to your children. We can bring that attitude to all kinds of troubles that might seem big as they're looming up in front of us but which experience tells us may well turn out to be nothing. This isn't the same as repressing our anxiety; we have to confront it to get through it. It's important for us to check in and ask ourselves, *Do I truly need to be worried about this?* If the problem is more concrete—you're about to be laid off, for instance—then you should get yourself some help and support so that you're better able to deal with it and less likely to transmit your anxiety to your kids.

A thirteen-year-old client of mine became very upset when she heard her parents discussing money problems. It blew up to massive proportions in her imagination; not only was she worried that her parents were going under but also about how she would ever be able to support herself as an adult. That nobody was talking to her about any of it made her that much more certain the situation was really dire. Her parents brought her to see me because they were worried about her. They didn't know that she was worried about them.

DON'T BE AFRAID TO SEEK HELP.

Don't be afraid to get outside help and support for you and your children if your problems threaten to overwhelm you. After all, if you want to be a teacher, you go to school and learn how to teach. If you're going to fly a plane, you get training for that. But there's not much training required to be a parent, and kids don't come with a manual. It takes courage, but it's important to seek help when you need it.

If you have something that you need to talk about with your kids, pay attention to how and where you're doing it. If a grandparent has passed away, you clearly can't hide that from them. How do you deliver that kind of news in the least upsetting way?

It helps to prepare by thinking through the kinds of questions your kid is likely to ask you about the situation and preparing your answers accordingly. This kind of conversation will probably be easier for you both to handle while you're on a walk or taking a drive. As

I've said earlier, kids often aren't comfortable with eye contact when discussing something really serious or awkward, so having the conversation while you can both be looking at other things is a good option.

Especially with young children, we have a tendency to soft-pedal bad news to make it more palatable, but you have to be careful about how you explain things. If you tell your kids, "Grandma went to sleep," then *they'll* worry that they're going to die every time they go to bed. Simply be truthful and say, "Grandma died." You need to consider the child's age and understanding when you're weighing the kind of language you want to use because kids will have different kinds of questions. If you have a good connection with your kids, you will know the level at which you can talk to them and what language to use so that they'll understand. You may want to have these talks individually if your children are not close in age.

Be prepared to answer whatever questions your kids may throw at you, understanding that those questions may be tough. If the topic is one that makes you uncomfortable, that will come across, and again, if you need help in knowing how to talk to your kid about it, look for help. Be honest. Again, if they're young, you probably don't need to share all of the details. But don't tell them something that isn't true, because they're likely to see through you. They're much sharper than we give them credit for.

DIVORCE IS TOUGH ON KIDS.

Divorce is a particularly hard topic to discuss with our kids because of how directly it affects them. Again, the best way to go into it is by being as prepared and as honest as you can be. A counsellor or coach can help you think through the way you tell the kids and what words to use, and it's best if both parents are there for the conversation. One of the most important things to cover is letting the kids know that it's not their fault. Children are highly egocentric and are likely to think that if Mom and Dad are getting a divorce, they must have done something to precipitate it. If they've been in trouble in the recent past—even a relatively small thing like failing a test—kids are especially likely to assume that's what drove you apart. Be sure to let them know up front that's not the case.

When dealing with a divorce, I believe that it's important to get outside help even if your kids seem to be adjusting well. They will often hide their true feelings from you because they don't want to create more problems. It's important that your kids be able to work through all the emotions they experience. Having their parents split up is a huge loss for kids. If they are not given the opportunity to work through it, it is very likely that issues will show up later, maybe even years down the road. Be proactive and get them support early on. This shows them that it is okay to ask for help and to work through emotions.

Kids are going to want to know what their new lives will look like. It's a good idea to ask them for their input, too. What are they most concerned about? Probably it's going to be where and with whom they'll be living. If you haven't worked that out, say so, but make sure your kids know that they'll always have a home and two parents who love them.

Divorce is tough on everyone, and you have to be aware of the feelings you're having, too. The concept is very similar to air-travel safety talk: You must put your own oxygen mask on first, because if you're not getting oxygen, then you're not going to be able to help anyone else. It's the same thing with our emotions. We need to constantly be checking in. How are we doing? And when the kids are reacting, showing that they're angry or confused or frightened by what they're hearing, we also need to be aware of how we're reacting to those emotions. Anger is a very common first response to news of a divorce, and if we're not prepared for that reaction, we may react in anger as well and lash out. We need to prepare ourselves and accept that, yes, our kids might be angry or sad. They might run out of the room. If we take time to think through the different scenarios that could play out, we can be ready to react in a reassuring way rather than creating more stress for our kids.

Again, divorce is a particularly complex scenario because of the firestorm of emotions it's likely to create. Very often when you're in the midst of a split, you're not sleeping well and are physically and emotionally exhausted. You may be angry with your spouse, or you may be so depressed that you can barely get out of bed. Again, I urge you to get help for yourself if you're feeling overwhelmed. Remember, we're role models for our kids. No matter what we're doing, whether it's how we take care of ourselves or how we handle stressful events, our kids are going to think that's what grown-ups do and conduct their lives accordingly.

THERE'S NOTHING SELFISH ABOUT SELF-CARE.

When my daughter was young, I was hypercareful about her care. I had lost a child at birth and was determined to be the best possible parent I could be for my other two children. We were in a playgroup where half of the moms would go out for coffee and the others would watch the children. I couldn't trust just anybody to look after my kids, so I always made sure my friend went with me so that we could split the childcare duties to ensure that our kids were well taken care of.

I remember that one of the mothers in the group was talking about a spa weekend she had planned for herself as a getaway and that she'd be leaving her toddler with the father. My initial reaction was how could she? How could this mother possibly leave her toddler for an entire weekend? This was something I thought I could never do. I had vowed to be the best mom I could possibly be. The idea of putting myself first seemed selfish. Yet, the truth is, when we take care of ourselves, we can be much better parents. If we are running on empty, we aren't much good to our kids or ourselves. It took me some time to learn this, but thankfully I did.

When I went through my divorce, a friend of mine said, "You really need to take care of yourself." There was a weeklong retreat that I really wanted to go on in Hawaii. Even thinking about it gave me tremendous guilt; how could I even contemplate going off to enjoy myself? Who would take care of my kids? But my friend insisted. "Say yes to this, then figure out the details afterwards." So I did; I found relatives to care for my children, packed my bag, and headed off for Hawaii, toting my guilt along with me—and it was the best thing I could possibly have done, not only for myself but for my children.

When I came home, I felt rejuvenated. I could handle the kids' meltdowns and all the other challenges I had to face so much more easily than before I left. The other beautiful discovery that came out of that experience was how well my kids did while I was gone. They had to do more for themselves than they would have had I been home, and they came through it beautifully and with more self-confidence in their coping abilities. They were excited to tell me the things that they had done and how they had managed. It was then that I fully realized, *Wow, this truly is a win-win.*

I continued to take those kinds of opportunities when they presented themselves, and I'm sure we were all better off having a less-stressed mom and more self-reliant kids around the house. We appreciated each other more for it, too; I loved coming home to hear, "Mom, I missed you. I'm so glad you're my mom."

There's enough guilt built into parenting without heaping it on ourselves for necessary self-care. And that self-care doesn't have to be a week in Hawaii; it can be little things like treating yourself to a bubble bath with candles or an evening out with a friend. The important thing is to commit to doing it and follow through.

KNOW WHEN YOU'VE HIT YOUR LIMITS.

Another piece of listening to and honouring your feelings is knowing when you've hit the limits of your patience and temper. If you're having a power struggle with your kid and you feel yourself losing your temper, sometimes it's best to walk away, lock yourself in the bathroom for five minutes, and then come back and deal with it. If we're angry, frustrated, or upset, then we're more likely to lash out at our kids in a way we'll regret later. Sadly, the negative things that we're liable to say when we lose our temper are the things that stay with and resonate for our kids for a long, long time. It takes a lot of positive reinforcement to wipe those things out, and no amount of regret on our part will make it better. It is better to take a cooling-off period than hurt the ones you love.

> Take a piece of paper and crumple it up; that takes just a moment. Now, try and spread it out so that the wrinkles don't show; that's next to impossible. That's very like the process of unsaying your harsh words.

Sometimes in the heat of the moment, we have these blinders on and can only see what's right in front of us. But if we can step back, take a breath, and remind ourselves about what's really important, we're less likely to lose our cool. When it's something like your kid not doing his homework, everyone getting angry, and dinnertime being imminent, just take five. If the homework doesn't get quite finished tonight, it's okay—just step back. It's more important that your family is able to sit down and enjoy dinner together. You can try again tomorrow. Or say your kid is running late for school and everybody's upset. Sometimes it's better to just phone the school and say, "My kid is going to be half an hour late." Take a few minutes and smooth things over, remind each other that you all love each other and things are okay, and then carry on with your day.

BEWARE OF OVERSHARING.

Whereas some parents are too withholding in terms of what they share about their emotional life with their kids, there are times when we may be tempted to share more than we should. A divorce usually brings with it a lot of anger, hurt, and frustration, and too often, kids get sucked into the vortex of the crumbling relationship or used as conduits between warring ex-spouses.

Don't let your anger or hurt feelings goad you into saying more about your ex to your children than you should.

Remember—to them, your ex is still a beloved parent. Love your kids more than you hate your ex, and don't turn them into unwilling pawns or force them to take sides. It only spreads the hurt around and damages everyone more than necessary. Telling your child, for instance, "Dad had an affair," is only going to hurt the child.

When you begin dating again, let your kids know about it as casually as you can. Don't expect them to be happy about it, but don't let that initial reaction upset you. It will take them time to get used to the idea. That said, this is certainly one of the times in your lives where outside help is called for, particularly for your kids. They're going to be struggling with their own feelings of anger and rejection and may be unwilling to discuss them with you. Finding a sympathetic professional for them to talk to can really help them work through their feelings in a constructive way.

When you start to date again, it may be tempting in the first flush of a new relationship to introduce your children to your potential partner. Don't be in a rush to bring your new friend home, though, because this can be hard on your children in ways you might not have considered. For one thing, children often fantasize about their divorced parents getting back together. You may know that's never going to happen, but they do often hold out these hopes, so for them it's painfully hard to see someone else stepping in their dad's or their mom's shoes. Wait until you're really getting serious before bringing them into the relationship. This is another time when getting outside help for your kids is important. They need to be able to work through their emotions.

START SMALL.

I went from feeling huge resistance to the thought of leaving my kids for a weekend to actually taking a weeklong retreat without them. It didn't happen overnight. When we don't take care of ourselves, it's easy to feel overwhelmed, resentful, and even angry. When we nurture ourselves, we can give from a place of love and peacefulness. If your life feels like it's been a treadmill of constant work or looking after kids, you're going to have to form this new habit slowly. Take one little step each week, and say, "This week, I'm going to take fifteen minutes for myself." Any of us can certainly take fifteen minutes, no matter how full our calendars are. Whether it's fifteen minutes of walking or fifteen minutes of quietly enjoying a book, make that happen on a regular basis.

TRY IT: TAKE TIME FOR YOU

Schedule fifteen minutes or more for yourself this week. Record when you'll do it and what you're going to do. Commit to it, and follow through. Partner with a friend and hold each other accountable for taking at least fifteen minutes for yourselves each week.

Ask for help if you need it. Whether it's with carpooling, swapping childcare, or even getting together with a friend to prepare a few meals to see you through the coming week, it's not going to happen if you don't let people know you want and need help.

And don't put off your self-care. When our kids are sick, we make the time to take them to the doctor. If they have a toothache, we'll drop everything to get them to the dentist. We have to get into the habit of prioritizing our own needs in the same way. It is important to take care of ourselves not only so that we can do what we need to do but also because our kids are watching us for cues. We can tell them, "You should eat healthy foods," but if we don't do that, they won't either. It's the same with self-care; we don't want our kids to be worn out, exhausted, not eating, not sleeping, and not getting outside and getting fresh air. We want them to take care of themselves, so we need to set that example.

I suggested earlier that keeping a baby picture of your teenager out where you can see it is often a good reminder to you of just how precious that child is to you, of how much you've always loved him or her and always will. Here's another suggestion: Take one of your own baby pictures and set it out where you'll see it often. You, too, are a precious being, someone who deserves joy, love, and time for yourself. That baby picture will remind you of that and of how much you mean to those who love you.

TRY IT: PHOTO MEMORIES

Place baby pictures of you and your children where you will see them often as a reminder that you and your children deserve joy, love, and time for yourselves. When your children look at the baby photos, share stories about when they were younger and when you were younger—they will love it!

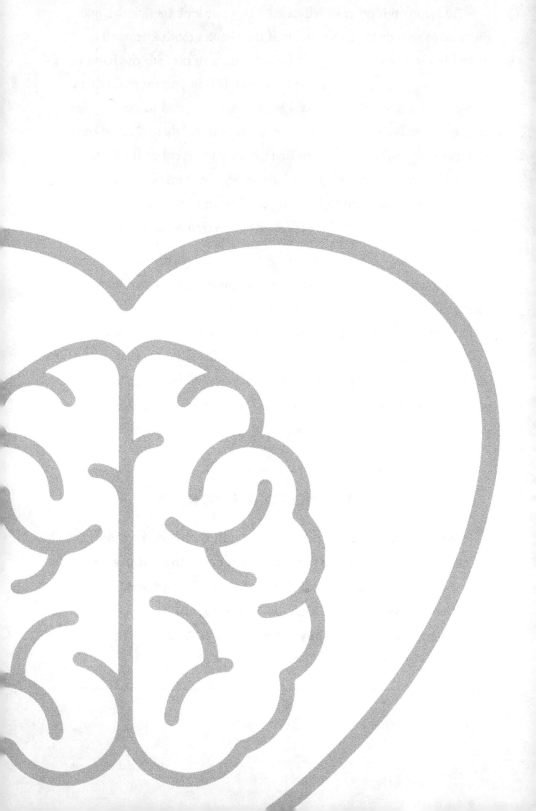

CHAPTER SEVEN

EASY WAYS TO REDUCE BULLYING

It seems like every other parenting piece I read is focused on the epidemic of bullying, and it's certainly a concern of many of the families in my practice. Is your child a target? Parents often tell me that the schools are unresponsive to their pleas for help or protection for their kids. It's heartbreaking to think about our kids at the mercy of unkind or even violent peers, but what can we do about it? Can we help our children to become "bully-proof"?

Kids who lack confidence and self-esteem are the most likely to be targeted because bullies look for some kind of power over others and can sense when another child feels powerless. I think that most of the time, bullies are kids who are missing something and feeling empty inside; by bullying, they are trying to get that something from somebody else. When I work with children who are the victims of bullying, building confidence and self-esteem is where I start.

One of my clients was a six-year-old boy who was being picked on every day at school. I had him close his eyes and led him through an exercise in which he visualized himself shielded inside a bubble, one that the bully wouldn't be able to break. When kids learn to do that, it shifts the energy in their body. They have a sense of being protected, so they feel braver, and that changes both their body language and the way that they react. The following week he came back to see me, and he said, "Guess what? All the kids are being nice to me." It can happen that quickly when you teach them to harness that inner energy.

Another client was a girl of nine; she told me that there was a girl who was always mean to her at school and said hurtful things. Again, I used a visualization exercise; I had her ground herself and then wrap herself in light for protection. We had met before the Christmas holidays, and a few days after she'd gone back to school, she came to see me. Now, she reported, this girl was actually leaving her alone. But she was bothered by the fact that the bully had turned her attention to other girls and was picking on them.

We talked about the reasons why kids bully, and I explained that they feel empty and alone. I talked with her about one of my favourite books, *Have You Filled a Bucket Today?* by Carol McCloud, which presents us with an imaginary bucket that we each have inside us that holds our feelings. The book explains that a bully has an empty bucket and how when we're nice to others—when we say "Thank you" or do something kind for them—it helps fill that other person's bucket as well as our own. I said, "If you can find it in your heart, if it feels right for you, then maybe you could concentrate on sending love from your heart to hers." She liked that idea and promised to try it.

The next week she came back and she said, "Guess what happened? She offered me candy, and she was being nice to people!" When we arm kids in this way to deal with bullying, we're taking the power out of the bully's hands and giving it back to the victim.

Another piece of this antibullying approach is reminding kids to fill their own buckets, too, and encouraging them in positive self-talk and visualization. There's more to this than you might think, in terms of science and physiology; research shows that our brain waves can synchronize with another person's heart rhythm up to five feet away.[2] Our emotions literally affect those around us, which is why it's important that we pay attention to what we're "broadcasting" to others. We may assume that our brain controls everything, but our heart plays a big part too.

Our electromagnetic field isn't just generated by our brains; the heart's magnetic field is actually sixty times stronger than that produced by our brain waves.[3] Our positive emotions have been shown to increase our emotional stability and mental sharpness so that when we are feeling compassionate or loving, those feelings affect our heart and create a more balanced heart rhythm. Emotions like anger or anxiety create a more erratic and unbalanced rhythm that sends out waves others can sense. That's why if kids are anxious and fearful and there's a bully around, the bully unconsciously picks up on those feelings, so those are the kids that they will prey on.

---

2 Rollin Mccarty, PhD, Raymond Trevor Bradley, PhD, and Dana Tomasino, BA, "The Heart Has It's Own 'Brain' and Consciousness," in5d, January 10, 2015, http://in5d.com/the-heart-has-its-own-brain-and-consciousness/.

3 P.J. Roach and M.S.Markov, editors, *Clinical Applications of Bioelectromagnetic Medicine* (New York: Marcel Dekker, 2004), 541–562.

WORDS DO MATTER.

This brings us back to the importance of how we as parents and teachers speak to children, because our words affect what's in their "buckets" and how they perceive themselves.

If you're saying to your kid, "You're lazy," or a teacher says something to a student that makes him feel bad about himself, it's going to affect his heart rhythm, release stress hormones, and create all kinds of havoc in his body. All of this makes it more likely that a bully will sense that your child is a potential victim, so it's vitally important that parents, teachers, and coaches—whoever may be working with our kids—are giving positive messages. Your body is like a drum, vibrating along with your emotions and thoughts. Make sure that you're playing the right music.

Unfortunately, we don't always give kids the tools they need to work their way through the world. I'm a big believer in tool kits for kids: something concrete that they can learn to rely on in times of stress or need. One of the things that I do for my clients is to create a personal CD with positive affirmations on it. I also encourage them to use crystals to help to lift their energy. Amethyst is a good one for that, obsidian helps to deflect negative energy, and clear quartz breaks up negative energy. I keep crystals at my office and will let kids choose what they want, then they can carry it with them in their backpack or put it in their pocket. Parents, if you take your child to a store where they sell crystals and let them choose for themselves, they will intuitively know and choose what they need. It's interesting to me that children nearly all love to collect rocks; we may assume it's just their natural curiosity about the world, but in my view, there's more to it than that. Every sort of rock vibrates a little bit differently and in ways that can be helpful.

Having warm baths with sea salts is another way to help clear energy. If a child is spending her days in a classroom where the teacher's yelling and there's a lot of negative stuff going on, she will come home carrying that energy with her. Kids today are so empathic; they really do feel other people's emotions and energy out there, so it's great to have a way to clear that energy.

TEACHING POSITIVE SELF-TALK

How do we teach our kids to speak to themselves in a way that will fill their "buckets" with powerful, positive messages? So much of this is forming the habit; most of us are engaged in self-talk all the time, but we're not really thinking about what the messages are that we're sending.

The first step is to sit down with the child and discuss the idea: "Let's stop and think. What's going through your head right now?" That can take a while because children (and adults) are often distracted and scattered. At this point I suggest that they close their eyes, breathe, tune into their bodies, and go within: "Just ask your body what's going on."

After a few quiet moments, sometimes the child will say something like, "I can feel my stomach." We focus on what that feeling is; what is his body telling him with this feeling? Then he's able to focus and say, for instance, "Well, I'm stressed about this math test." When I ask him what he's worried about, he'll tell me, "I'm not very good at math." This is the first step for the child—

paying attention to his feelings, hearing that negative thought that's taken root in his mind, and voicing it.

This is the point at which we flip the script: "Let's change that to, 'I am good at math. I learn math easily.'" The fact is, if we think that we're not good at something, we won't be. Pulling out the weed of self-doubt and replacing it with the seeds of self-confidence creates the sense of hopefulness and possibility that kids need to succeed. Henry Ford said it best: "Whether you think you can or you think you can't—you're right." And once kids can internalize positive thoughts, those thoughts become the truth.

But you're going to have weeds popping up in your garden, so caring for it has to be a daily exercise. You can't stop negative thoughts from sprouting up, but you can keep them from taking over. Keeping the negative thoughts at bay creates more room for the good thoughts to come through and gives them the chance to grow and get stronger. As time goes by, you'll see fewer and fewer weeds coming in. When you feel yourself backsliding to negativity, be aware of it, and proactively get it out of your head and off your "loop" of self-talk.

Helping your children make this kind of change in their thinking isn't difficult, especially if they're younger. Once they're aware of it, they'll notice it in themselves and in you, too. I worked with one young client to help her with her self-talk about her appearance. When she heard her mother complaining about how fat she was, my client told her, "Mom, Nola says we need to talk nicely to ourselves."

TRY IT: BAN NEGATIVE TALK

Ban negative talk in your home for an entire week. Hold each other responsible and recognize when family members say something negative about themselves or anyone else. Have a jar or small plastic pail or bucket for each family member. When someone says something negative about themselves, help them by writing a positive affirmation and placing it in his or her "bucket." At the end of the week, or the end of each day, each person can read his or her positive affirmations aloud to the family. Maybe you want to create a new ritual and share a positive affirmation every morning or evening.

The process is about creating awareness: the daughter picked up that Mom was not talking nicely to herself and that she needed to change it. Another young client had been bullied so badly that her parents opted to pull her out of her school and put her into another one. With my help, she developed a new, more positive way of talking to herself about her strength, her bravery, and her ability to handle tough situations. Her problems with bullies evaporated when she took control of her self-talk.

FLIPPING THE SCRIPT

Sometimes it takes a bit more time for kids to realize the extent to which they're generating negative thoughts about themselves. I sometimes ask clients, "Do you ever say negative things about yourself?" and they'll insist that they don't. The fact is, we all do it, but it's so habitual that we don't "hear" ourselves anymore. When I run up against that, I ask them to think of a situation in the past— perhaps when they were bullied or their parents were upset with them—to close their eyes, remember that situation, and get in touch with how they felt in that moment. Once they connect with how it felt, I say, "Okay. Where do you feel it in your body?" The answer is usually something like, "My heart feels heavy," or "My chest hurts."

"Okay. What do you think you're saying to yourself right now?" That's usually when the feelings come out. "Mom's upset with me. I spilled something, and I made a mess. I'm so clumsy."

"Is that really the truth? You spilled something once, but that doesn't make you clumsy. Are you like that 100 percent of the time?"

"No."

"Okay. Do you never spill anything?"

"No. Sometimes I do."

I said, "Okay. So which thoughts are you going to choose? Because you have a choice about what thoughts go through your head." With younger kids I'll use the image of a garden to help them visualize how to root out the bad thoughts. With teens, I talk about the crawl of words that appears on the television screen below a newscast, explaining how the words that appear there are like the loop that plays in their heads and influences how they look at the world and at themselves.

A great exercise I like to do with my clients is having them meditate or visualize as I guide them. I have them close their eyes, take three or four deep breaths, and then visualize a place that feels comfortable and they would love to be. It could be someplace that they've been on vacation; it could be in their room, if that's where they feel safe; or they can make up a fantasy world of unicorns and mountains made out of whipped cream. They are only limited by their imaginations. I guide them to pay attention to what is there and who is there. I'll say, "Is there somebody else there with you? Do they have a message for you?" Sometimes they'll tell me, "Yeah, 'You need to be nice to yourself.'" It's very interesting what they'll come up with. I'll get them to draw what it is that they saw so that they can take it home and have that as something to remember: "I need to be good to myself. I need to be saying these things to myself and remember not to let the negative things stay in my head."

This is harder for adults; we don't often listen to the positive messages trying to break through in our heads. But kids are far more tuned-in and open to their inner guidance or the positive thoughts they hear in their head, so it's not so hard for them to access them. They usually respond quickly with the positive messages or thoughts. My clients learn to use their inner guidance or wisdom in all kinds of creative, positive ways. One of them, a boy of eleven, told me how he'd been stymied by how to tackle a school project until he took the time to close his eyes, relax, and listen to himself as I'd taught him. He said that when he did, ideas and mental pictures just flowed out of him, and he whipped through the assignment in record time.

SELF-CARE IS CRITICAL.

When I'm working with kids, I also work with parents, because kids often reflect the thoughts and energy they're getting at home. If, as so many parents are, they're stressed about finances or their jobs, then all of that stress and energy are being put out into their homes, and kids are picking up on that. That also goes for teachers and for coaches who work with children: if they're stressed in the classroom or the gym, their energy is affecting all of the students in their orbit. The question becomes: What can you do to relax and help change so that you're sending out positive energy and your heart rhythms are balanced and calm? For adults, as with kids, it's about taking time to meditate or do some yoga or visualizations. They must become aware and make a conscious choice.

TRY IT: QUICK CALMING IDEAS

- Take four nice, deep breaths.

- Put your hand over your heart and focus on your breathing for a couple minutes.

- Listen to an upbeat song.

- Move your body: take a quick stretch or walk.

- Tense all your muscles, hold for ten to fifteen seconds, and then relax.

- Have a glass of water.

- Look out the window—notice the beauty in nature.

- Hug yourself.

- *Smile!*

I know parents and teachers are busy, but you can make time to go in the bathroom and take two minutes to do some deep breathing, because even something as simple as this helps to slow your heart rate and bring your blood pressure down right away, and that will make a difference for the kids around you. It's not a big effort on your part, but it is one that will pay off for both you and your kids.

I've talked about the importance of self-care for parents, and this is another area in which investing some time will pay off for your kids; go for a walk outside in nature, or spend some time meditating, doing yoga, or whatever it is that fills you up and relaxes you. Make time to play the active sports you enjoy or just to take a long, hot bath. You're not only setting the tone for the exchanges between you and the world, but you're also setting a positive example and being a role model for your kids.

WHAT IF *YOUR* KID IS THE BULLY?

What happens when you get that dreaded call from school that your child has wilfully hurt someone or is picking on them? It happens, and it's important to understand the whys on the other side of the bullying interaction if we're going to help kids move past this.

I've recently been working with a fourteen-year-old girl whose parents came to me because their daughter had been harassing and physically intimidating another girl at school. In talking with her, I discovered that she was having issues with her self-confidence. Reading was tough for her, and kids had been making fun of her for that. She was struggling with friendships. She'd withdrawn into herself, not wanting to do anything or interact. She'd felt that the other girl was in her face, and her "fight-or-flight" reaction kicked in, because her personal space was all she had, and she was going to defend it. When we're stressed all the time, that's what happens. We're not clearly thinking about our actions. We just react.

We talked about that, and I said, "What can you do next time if someone's getting into your space? How do you prepare for it?" We did some deep breathing exercises and that helped her to become more calm and centred. We talked about the feelings she'd had before she hit the girl. We talked about how being hit must have felt to the girl she'd attacked.

Finally I said, "Yes, you were protecting yourself, and it was a reaction, but now you're being seen as a bully," and that wasn't what she wanted. We began to plan for what she could do differently the next time, to have a better outcome. "How can you be in a calm place and be in control of how you react to this girl? Maybe you could just say, 'You're getting too close. Please back away.'" We also worked on her image of herself as someone who couldn't learn and wasn't bright.

Middle school is a tough time for nearly everyone, but she's making progress and is doing better in her reading, too. Kids can be hurtful and insensitive at times, so my work with her is centred on helping her feel better about herself. It's a process of constant building because you can build kids up, but then something happens again at school, and it can bring them down unless they are really strong. She has some coping strategies now: "I can do some deep breathing. I can move away. I can ask the teacher for help." It's essential for kids with issues like these to go in with a plan because if she's clear on the plan and committed to following it, then when the next person invades her space or pushes her buttons in some way, there's a better chance that she'll choose a different coping strategy and won't reflexively lash out.

Dealing with having a child who's bullying others is tough on parents, and often we just don't know what to say or how to react. We're angry; we're also embarrassed by what the child has done, conscious on some level that it can be seen as a reflection of our parenting. What will people think of him? What will they think of us? We feel judged. We're liable to lash out at them and take a hostile, combative tone that puts the blame on him before we've heard his side of it. But when you talk to your child about it, the key again is listening without judgment and being willing to hear your child's story. What's going on under the surface?

In order to find out, we have to be willing to step back, take some deep breaths, and prepare to listen to our kid's side. Instead of saying, "How could you hit somebody? What were you thinking?" try for a more neutral, "I heard from the school today. Tell me what happened."

Your success in getting your child to open up to you in a situation as stressful and emotionally fraught as this will hinge to some extent on the openness of your relationship in the past. If you haven't been communicating for a while, it will take longer to get this dialogue going. But stick with it. When your child tells you what the other kid, in his perception, did to him to precipitate his action, your best response is, "Oh. No wonder you were angry." When you've established that calm, low-stress dialogue, you can talk about the future and what ideas he has for how to respond in a different way should the situation arise again.

When we are stressed, we go to that reptilian brain, and it's fight-or-flight. When a child's brain is telling him to protect himself—*boom*—he will likely punch or push without even thinking. Telling him they can't do that doesn't help solve the underlying problem that pushed him to that response in the first place. What is your kid feeling about himself? What stresses made him feel cornered in that situation?

Usually what's underneath is some kind of hurt: They're not getting attention or they're afraid. Matching their anger with your own won't help the situation, so don't rise to the bait if they're initially contentious or combative. If you feel yourself getting angry, simply say, "I think we need to cool down a little. I'm going to step away for a few minutes, and then we can try again." Go to your room, take a few deep breaths, and come out when you're ready to continue more calmly.

It's certainly right to expect to be treated and talked to with respect, but again, we need to do that for our kids, not just lash back at them, saying, "Go to your room. You're always angry, and I can't deal with you." Now isn't the moment that you want to inflict new pain on your child or say things that can't be unsaid. Walk away if you have to. Get a spouse or somebody to step in for a little bit if you need to, but don't say things you'll regret. Anger begets anger, and the old saying, "A soft voice turns away wrath," is a wise one.

What motivates bullies? It may be that their teacher or other kids have said something that really hurt them, or they are feeling like they don't matter and are scared. When somebody walks by them and looks at them the wrong way, that's the last straw, and they lash out at that kid. Almost always, when kids bully, we find that underneath the outburst is pain, fear, or shame. Somehow the idea is that by bringing someone lower, you will be higher—that if you take a kid's money or lunch or humiliate him, you will be seen as a powerful person rather than the powerless person you fear you are. Bullies' buckets are empty; they have no positive sense of themselves.

The bottom line is that whether your children are the bullies or the bullied, the best way to break that cycle is to give them a strong sense of themselves, to fill that bucket with alternatives to feeling powerless and with strategies to cope with the stresses that brought on the situation in the first place.

LET KIDS KNOW YOU BELIEVE IN THEM.

Everyone needs to feel that they matter. Everyone needs to have some sense of control around their world and their choices. That's why I urge parents to avoid taking an authoritarian, dictatorial attitude toward their kids and to avoid laying down the law when the kids are old enough to reason things out for themselves. Teach them to think through the consequences of their actions ahead of time. If they don't turn their homework in tomorrow, what will be the outcome of that? Let them work through it with gentle prompting.

"I won't be prepared for my test, and I might fail it."

"Is that what you want?"

"Well, no."

"So what are you going to do?"

"I guess go back to my homework."

This gives ownership of his actions and their outcomes back to your child: "I'm choosing to study right now because I want to do well on this test. Not because Mom or Dad is telling me to study or because the teacher said I had to. I'm choosing to do it."

It's important to let your kids know that you believe in them and support them. Give them strategies and tools to feel more confident and resilient rather than telling them what to do.

My own daughter was being bullied a few years ago, and I found the advice the school was giving her to be ineffective: "Just don't let it bother you. Be more resilient." But just telling children to be more resilient without helping them find ways to do it or, worse, planting negativity isn't much help. Kids look up to adults and crave their attention. This is why it is so important for teachers and others who work with kids to watch their words and avoid labelling kids negatively and shrinking their self-esteem. Teachers need to take a moment to focus on what kids did right; yes, maybe they failed a test, but if they got even a couple of answers correct, use that to encourage them and point out that victory, no matter how small. They will strive harder and will feel more able and competent—and resilient.

If we build kids up and believe in them, they'll rise to that benchmark because when a parent or teacher or coach believes in kids, they will work harder.

Teachers, try doing the gratitude exercise with your kids. Let each child in class tell everyone something for which he or she is grateful to another student, whatever it is. Kindness is a mind-set and a habit; kids who are reminded to be kind will make a habit of it.

SIBLINGS FIGHT.

Sibling rivalry is a fact of family life. It can range from very mild to very destructive. That rivalry can lead to intrafamily bullying, with the bigger or older kid usually making the smaller sibling his or her victim. How can we as parents put the brakes on this kind of interaction?

Unfortunately, parents often provide the fuel for rivalry, usually by trying to pit the kids against each other to create a positive competition. But remarks like "Your brother is so smart and always practices without me reminding him," translate to "Mom thinks my brother is better than I am," in your kid's head, and that's not at all the message you want your kid to internalize.

Break the habit of comparing your kids to each other, as it will only breed conflict between them. Be aware of what you say and how you say it. Keep what comes out of your mouth as positive, loving, and encouraging as you can. Don't pull one child down to prop another up, and don't praise one kid at the expense of a brother or sister. This will help create a more harmonious home.

If you carve out time to spend with each kid individually, you're letting him or her know that you see all your children as unique, lovable, worthy individuals who you appreciate for their own merits. You may think you can motivate them by pitting them against each other, but what comes of that isn't likely to be the outcome you were hoping for.

When you listen to your children, give them your time and patient understanding, and enjoy them for who they are—you'll see less sibling rivalry.

Focus on the words that you're using and use them to create a positive environment. Your kids will feel better about themselves and will be more cooperative and helpful; the fighting and jostling will stop; and you'll be moulding a family that enjoys each other's company and respects each other's individuality.

I can hear parents saying, "One more thing to do?!" I get it, but I'm not talking about a major time commitment here. A lot can be accomplished in tiny, five-minute exchanges. If you come home and find that your teen has unloaded the dishwasher without being asked or has already started dinner for you, make sure to praise him, hug him, and tell him how much you appreciate it. When your kids see that their efforts mean something to you, they'll be happy to do even more.

It makes a big difference. It's so worth it to create wonderful relationships with your kids; to be able to work together as a family and have fun, too; to put on music when you come home and dance around while you're all cooking dinner together. It's just a matter of acting intentionally rather than reacting to every little thing without thinking through how your reaction will be perceived.

BUILD RESILIENCE.

It breaks my heart when I hear parents say that they're counting the days until their kids are old enough to move out of the house, or, "Yeah, I love my kids, but I don't really like them." It doesn't have to be that way. And I do understand; I'm not perfect either. Who hasn't had a conversation that starts with your kid saying, "You don't have time for me," and we react with, "What do you mean? I cook, and I clean, and I drive you places."

Instead of reacting, what we need to do is think what's behind that thought; are they asking for something they need that we're not hearing—perhaps time beyond the chore-driven interactions we usually have? Imagine if your spouse reacted to you saying, "We don't spend enough time together," by replying, "I go to work every day and bring home the money." What would you want your spouse to understand? "I want to have time. I want to sit and have a glass of wine with you tonight and talk about our day. That's what's important to me."

It's the same thing for kids; they want time spent with you that's meaningful for them, making memories that will say to them, "Mom cares," or "Dad cares," or "Dad made time for me because he came out and played hockey with me for twenty minutes." It's also important that we take the time to hear what it is that is meaningful for our kids—not just for us. Maybe your kid doesn't really want to spend his one-on-one time shooting hoops, for instance. Check in and ask him directly, "Tell me what you want, not what you don't want or what I'm doing wrong. Be specific and say, 'This is what I want from you,' or 'This is what I need from you right now,' so I'll know." Then be open to hearing what he has to say.

Don't hesitate to be clear about what you want and need as well, because your kids may not always intuit it: "Right now, Mom has a migraine, and I need you to be quiet. And then, when it's gone, we can go and have an ice cream together." Having that communication, asking for what we want, and teaching our kids to do the same is vitally important to happiness in relationships of all kinds. What they want from us may be as simple as sitting down for a cup of tea with them, but we won't know unless we ask.

The children we raise will go out in the world with what we've given them, and that will dictate to a large extent how well they cope and how they treat others. Bullies, whose low self-esteem makes them search for control or dominance over others, will go on being bullies. We don't want to raise bullies, and we don't want to raise kids who'll grow up without the self-esteem and inner resources to reject being made a victim of bullies. Help your children understand their own needs, and fill their buckets. Help them see that bullying comes from weakness and fear, not from strength.

Encouraging our kids to take ownership of their reactions and feelings puts the power into their hands and helps them become more confident and resilient. We always have a choice in how we view things, and thus, how we feel. Finding the bright side in tough times helps us to move through situations much easier. Teaching our kids this important lesson will help them feel a sense of control over their life and be much less likely to lash out or blame others.

CHAPTER EIGHT

UNDERSTANDING DEPRESSION IN CHILDREN

C hildren and teens can experience depression. Depression is something no parent wants to have to deal with. It's frightening, and the diagnosis can make us feel angry and powerless. But it's far more dangerous to brush it off or to ignore the symptoms that might point to depression. Kids, especially adolescents, are known for their moodiness and hormonal swings. It's easy to chalk up their behaviours to that and miss important warning signs.

Teens can present their symptoms differently than adults. We think of the typical person with depression as being withdrawn and feeling sad all the time, but depression can also manifest as anger and lashing out. Depression often manifests in physical symptoms like headaches, stomachaches, or general aches and pains—you take them to doctors and they can't find anything wrong. Depressed kids can be extremely sensitive to criticism. Problems at school, running away, and drug and alcohol abuse are all ways that kids may signal depression. Sometimes they withdraw from some people but not all.

WHAT ARE COMMON SIGNS OF DEPRESSION IN KIDS?

Internet addiction or playing video games all the time are sometimes symptomatic of depression because those are ways to shut out the world. Sometimes a change in the way that they dress is a signal, or they may change their friends and start hanging out with different people.

Kids with depression often lose interest in the things they used to like. Sleep habits can shift too, either to insomnia or to sleeping longer hours. Often, teens love to sleep in; if your kid starts sleeping more, that could be because of hormones and changes in melatonin levels, but it could also be a sign of depression.

Kids and teens struggling with depression will often change their eating and exercise habits and will have weight gain or weight loss. They may be eating to try to cover up their feelings or losing weight because of a loss of interest in food. Sometimes, kids with anorexia or bulimia struggle with depression as well. Many kids with depression will get into alcohol or drug use as a way to self-medicate—anything to dull the pain that they're feeling.

Self-harm in the form of cutting is very common. I've known kids as young as nine who cut. They'll often hide it. If they're cutting on their arms, they'll wear long sleeves or a bunch of bracelets around their wrist to cover it up. They'll cut their upper thigh or their abdomen so parents don't see that. If it's summertime and you see your kid is wearing long sleeves, that's something to pay attention to. One girl started wearing shorts for swimming instead of her bathing suit because she'd started cutting her thighs.

Even though it's uncomfortable, we need to start talking about suicide. Kids with suicidal thoughts often give out warning signs. A kid who's depressed and may be contemplating suicide might give away prized possessions. Sometimes, kids will express their feelings in art; one girl drew a picture of a girl with tears running down her face and tape over her mouth, which signalled to me that she didn't feel as though she had a voice. Suicide is a very real danger with kids, as awful as that is to contemplate. They often warn us, but we sometimes don't listen or brush what they're saying aside, assuming they're just being dramatic. Don't. If your kid is saying things like, "I wish I was dead," or "People would be better off without me," or "When I'm gone . . ." they're trying to hand you a clue.

People with suicidal thoughts don't really want to die, yet they fall into thinking that's the only way out when things get really bad. They'll often throw little hints out to you to let you know that something is going on, if you're paying attention.

BE WATCHFUL FOR CHANGES IN BEHAVIOUR.

When we think about teens, among the first words that come to mind is "moody." Part of that is normal behaviour because their job as teens is to become independent of us. There's often internal struggle because they want to be independent, yet it's scary, so they still want to have their parents' input. It's a back-and-forth thing that creates a lot of stress.

If you start to see your teen behaving in a way that's out of the ordinary, though, don't be too quick to write it off. It may be nothing, but it's certainly worth checking out and asking about it. I think sometimes parents are afraid to ask, thinking, *I don't want to make it worse.* Or, as one mom told me, she didn't want to face the fact that it might be a bigger deal than just typical teenage behaviour. If your kid has been really mopey, you may be worrying, *Are they suicidal? Are they having suicidal thoughts?* but be too afraid to ask, thinking, *I don't want to push them over the edge.*

Ask. It really is important to ask the question, and it's okay to ask it. If kids aren't thinking about suicide, they'll say, "No, I'm not." Asking is not going to encourage them to commit suicide, much less suggest that it's somehow a good idea, so don't worry about putting the thought into their heads. It's worth asking them what's going on if you're worried and if they're moping around. Have that conversation, and see what they tell you. Everyone has a down day or two, but if the moping goes on for a couple of weeks, you're right to become concerned and to address it by having that discussion.

Parents, you know your kids best. If they're moody for even a couple days, obviously there's something going on. If they're not depressed, it may just be that maybe they had a fight with their best friend. Maybe something happened at school, maybe they've just broken up with their girlfriend or boyfriend, or maybe something else occurred and they're sad and need some support. Any of these things is all the more reason to ask, to listen, and to have that conversation.

If it's not turning around after a couple of weeks, then it's certainly time to get some help. It's worth having kids go and see the doctor or to talk with a therapist or a coach who works with kids or teens, is familiar with depression, and can act to help them so it doesn't get worse. It may take several attempts to find the right person; teens must connect with the therapist or coach. Don't assume they are just being difficult. It has to be the right match in order for them to feel comfortable with being open. Also, make sure to tell teens that you're not trying to "fix them," only to get them the support they need to move through life's struggles. Adults struggling with depression can sometimes find the strength to pick up the phone and seek out the help they need because they know where to get it. Teens often don't. Many people with depression don't even know that it's not normal to feel that way. It can start very gradually, with stress at school or not having friends and feeling down. It just keeps going on and on. Then it starts to feel normal. They don't know it's supposed to be different.

There is help out there. It's important that parents are paying attention and are willing to say, "I've noticed that you've been really down and mopey for a couple of weeks. Let's make an appointment with the doctor and go in and talk to him." If your child has worked with a psychologist or therapist in the past, then you can say, "It's time to go and see so-and-so again. I've noticed you seem to be unhappy more often."

THE CONSEQUENCES OF IGNORING DEPRESSION CAN BE DEVASTATING.

The idea of a young person taking his or her life is so horrific, so unthinkable, that we often push it aside, yet suicide is the second-leading cause of death in young people in Canada, and the third-leading cause of death among the young in the United States. Over the last thirty years, suicide and attempted suicide have increased 300 percent. Nine out of ten suicides take place in the home. For every completed suicide, there are an estimated thirty to fifty attempts.[4] And it's not just teens who get depressed; even six- or seven-year-olds can suffer from it.

A BAD CHOICE CAN SPIRAL INTO A WORSE ONE.

I worked with a teenaged girl who was suicidal because she had taken a nude photo of herself and texted it to her boyfriend, who had shared it on social media. She was devastated, humiliated, and panicked. In her culture, this meant that she had brought shame to the entire family. She felt there was no way out, so she took a bunch of Tylenol, trying to kill herself. Fortunately it just made her sick. I was volunteering at a high school when she came and talked to me. She couldn't promise me that when she went home, she wasn't going to attempt to kill herself again. I had to call her mom and have her mom take her to the hospital. Her mother was initially disinclined to take it seriously, and I had to insist that this was literally her daughter's life on the line.

I think that's something we as parents tend to do; if our kids say they want to die, it's easy to dismiss it as drama and to respond with, "Don't be silly. You've got so much to live for." You list all of their advantages and blessings: "You've got a home to live in. You've got food to eat. There are people out there that are starving. You should be grateful for all that you have." But that's exactly the wrong way to go, and that will only make it worse. That will push them further into the isolation they're feeling, certain now that their own parents don't even understand them: "I tried to tell them, but they don't

---

4 Canadian Mental Health Association, 2016, http://www.cmha.ca/.

listen. I don't have any friends at school. I'm failing. I'm stupid. My parents aren't getting it. They don't understand me."

I remember talking to one young girl who was feeling suicidal and hopeless. She told me her mom literally pulled out a knife from the drawer and handed it to her daughter, saying, "Here. I'm tired of hearing about it." I think parents can get tired of hearing from kids that they're depressed, or they're sad, or things aren't going well. When they're constantly saying, "I wish I was dead. Everybody would be better off without me," then after a while, a parent can just throw up her hands and say, "I'm tired of hearing about it," like this one mom did. I'm not judging her; it is exhausting when your child is struggling for a long period of time. That is why it is so important for the parents to also get help.

We don't always have the answers for our own kids, and even though I had sympathy for this mom who was clearly at the end of her rope, you have to take it seriously and go and get the help your child needs, not just dare her to follow through. Sometimes parents will say, "They're just trying to get attention." Honestly, it's more that they are in so much pain that they can't see a way out. They just want it to stop. It is a cry for help, not for attention.

The fact is that most suicidal people, if they knew a way past the pain, if they could see the other side, wouldn't attempt to end their lives. But in the grip of depression, light just doesn't penetrate that far into their personal darkness. And depression can hit any of us, at any point in our lives. Even if we've had a good life and a stable upbringing, we can be knocked down by some cataclysmic event—a painful personal loss, a sudden turn of fortune—and simply lack the strength or resilience to bounce back. If we don't know how to handle those kinds of emotions, they can easily turn into depression and take us further and further down that dark road if we can't get, or don't have the will to find the help we need. Depression is not always caused by an external event. When kids compare themselves with their peers, celebrities, or social media posts, it can be easy to feel inferior. If the comparisons lead to a lot of negative self-talk, it can lead to depression. Depression can also be caused by some medications, genetics, concussions, and also the structure of the brain. If your child is struggling, it is important to get help. This is important to remember. It is not something they can just snap out of. They need support and care just as much as someone with a physical illness.

If your child has exhibited these behaviours . . .

- expressed the thought that the world would be better off without him, or that he wishes he was dead

- given away her prized possessions or made out some sort of will

- withdrawn from his previous interests or friends

- has lost interest in how she appears or in personal hygiene

- shows radical changes in sleeping or eating habits

- becomes angry frequently

. . . you need to address this directly and at once.

If your child talks about suicide, ask him directly: "Have you made a plan for this?" Kids who have will very often tell you so. If that's the case, get help immediately—even if it's dialling 911. Suicide prevention hotlines and crisis centres are also great sources for help.

If your child's answer is "No," then your response can be, "Let's put some things in place. If you're feeling really bad, I need you to promise me that you're going to talk to me, or talk to your dad, so we can help you through this." Give your child resources: "Do you know there are kids' help lines where you can talk to somebody if you don't feel you can tell me about it? There are other people you can talk to." Follow up with, "Let's set up an appointment with somebody for you to talk to."

Parents often assume that their children won't be frank with them if they ask if they're planning suicide, but surprisingly often, they will be. It takes courage to ask that question and to act. If your children are saying these things, don't leave them alone. Make sure they have someone who understands the gravity of the situation with them at all times.

DON'T BE AFRAID TO TALK TO YOUR CHILDREN.

You'll be surprised how much they may tell you if you ask them. If your kid is mopey, has lost interest in friends she used to like, and has stopped caring about what she looks like—talk to her and say, "I've noticed a change in you. You haven't been spending time with your friends lately. I'm concerned. What's going on?"

Listen to your children and give them a chance to open up. Listen without judgment. Sometimes they might be a failing a class at school, or they failed a test and they're used to getting good grades. That can be devastating. They may start thinking, I'm so stupid. *I'm not doing well at school.*

Again, it's easy for parents to want to step in and reassure them: "No, you're smart." But that's just going to shut them down. Instead, listen and acknowledge what they're saying. Speak up to validate their feelings, not to deny them: "You're not feeling good. You failed that test. That must be really tough." That's how to keep the conversation going. Let them vent, and don't contradict them or try to "buck them up," and they'll keep talking.

Don't be quick to give advice: "You failed that test. I guess you just need to study harder." That will just drag them down further. Your natural desire as a parent is to try and fix things for your kids, and I understand that it's coming from a place of love. We want to help, but that's not the way our kids will interpret it. They feel that we're passing judgment on them, even if that's not our intent. Remember, at this juncture your child is hypersensitive to criticism, whether real or imagined, and when Mom may mean to show her concern, what your child is hearing is that she's disappointed or angry. It's important to check in and make sure she's hearing what you meant to say: "How did you understand that?"

Your child may surprise you by answering, "You're just mad. You think I'm a failure. I'm a pain in the butt." That may not be at all what you were trying to get across to her, but that's the way she received it.

Sometimes that's really frustrating. As a parent you want her to understand, "Of course I'm concerned about you. I'm just trying to help." But if the way she's hearing it is not what you meant, it's your job to find a way to get her to understand what you were trying to get across.

Too often we don't stop to think that a young person doesn't have the life experience required to put things in perspective. For parents, if kids are upset about school or breaking up with a boyfriend or a friend, it's easy for us to say, "That's no big deal." But to our kids, it's huge. They don't know yet that they're going to get dumped a few times in their life and that initial heartbreak is devastating. Whatever it is, they can't see past it.

Remind them that it will get better and that their feelings will change no matter how bad things are right now. Sometimes they can't see past what they're going through in the moment: "I feel awful. There's so much pain. I don't know how I'll ever get past this. I can't face other people." Let them know you've been there, you understand, and there are always answers and a way to move forward.

Let them know you are there to support them. You are not judging. You're not going to lecture them. Let them know they're not alone in this. "I'm not going to let you go through this alone. I'm here to help you. Let's figure out together how we're going to get through it. If we need help, we'll get it."

HELP FOR DEPRESSION

There is a whole range of therapeutic options to deal with depression in young people, whether it's seeing a psychologist or working with someone like me. There are art therapists for kids who are creative. Teens do use antidepressants, although in my view it shouldn't necessarily be a first choice. Antidepressants are designed and tested for adults. The decision for your teen to take them needs to be carefully thought out and discussed by you, your child, and their doctor or psychiatrist. You have to find the right medication for your child; everybody reacts a bit differently to different medications. There are risks associated with antidepressants, but if that's what's going to save your kid's life, absolutely go for it. That said, medication alone should never be seen as the solution. Your child needs therapy and the tools with which to face future emotional challenges and setbacks. With those in place, your child may eventually be able to get off medication.

Antidepressants are designed and tested for adults. The decision for your teen to take them needs to be carefully thought out and discussed by you, your child, and their doctor or psychiatrist.

Other things can help in conjunction with medication and therapy. Outdoor exercise has been shown to be effective, in part because of the exposure to sunlight, which has the power to alter mood. You might also encourage your child to try listening to meditations (found on YouTube, iTunes, and similar sources), journaling, or doing something they love like playing an instrument, doing something creative, or spending time with friends, if he or she is up to it. Sitting by a sunny window or a light box is helpful for many, as is spending time with a pet or looking at family photos.

DON'T NEGLECT YOURSELF.

It's very stressful when kids are struggling with depression, especially if they're having suicidal thoughts—not just for them and you but also for the rest of your family. It's very important for parents to take care of themselves and their other kids. That stress in the home affects everybody there, so get the support you all need. If your child is going for therapy, it can't hurt for parents to go and get some support as well. "How do I best deal with this with my kid? How can I support my kid? How can I take care of myself?" are questions a good therapist can help you to answer.

It's easy to become totally focused on your kid's well-being; you're watching him or her all the time, so you forget to eat or sleep or do what you need to do to take care of yourself. Remember, if you're in bad shape emotionally, that's going to reverberate through the whole family. Don't be afraid to reach out to those who care for you to ask for their help or support, however you need it. If you need to go talk to a friend or get somebody to bring you meals, ask for that. It's not just about the teen with depression. It's everybody.

Things that might seem trivial to us as adults can be flashpoints for kids. I worked with an eleven-year-old boy who had gotten into a fistfight with a friend. His father was very angry, and as a punishment he took away his son's iPad, and somehow it got broken in the process. That probably doesn't sound like a devastating blow to you, but for that child, it seemed like the end of the world. That was where he kept his music, how he kept in touch with his friends, and how he did his art. He was a highly sensitive and creative kid who already had a hard time feeling like he fit in; his dad was very athletic and outdoorsy and liked to do active things that just didn't appeal to this boy. They weren't really close. Now he'd lost his conduit to the outside world, and with it, his will to live.

I could see that he was feeling really low. I said, "Are you wishing that you weren't here?" He admitted that he was. I asked him more about that, and he talked about feeling suicidal, although he didn't have a plan. His mother had brought him to see me, and I asked him, "Do you want me to talk to your mom, or would you like me to help you talk to her?" He chose to talk to her himself with me there. He said, "I'm feeling like ending my life."

We talked him through what he'd need to do to get a new iPad; he actually came up with this whole plan about how he could do extra chores and how he could go and shovel snow to earn the money to get it. He asked if it would be okay if he started doing these extra things so he could make extra money and, of course, his mom agreed. They actually had a great conversation. She was also willing to go and talk to the dad on his behalf, which was a great relief to the boy.

I heard from his mom a few days later. He'd brightened up now that he had hope and a plan of action. Sometimes all we need to survive is the light of hope. If you can help your child to lift his head and see that light, you can save his life.

IN CONCLUSION . . .

E veryone needs an emotional haven, someone with whom they feel safe to be open and authentically themselves. Parents, if you want your kids to be open and honest with you, to come to you with their concerns and problems, you need to provide that haven by offering unconditional love that doesn't judge or have an agenda. Just be there, letting them know that they're loved and that you're always there to help them to find the answers.

Support your kids in finding and exploring their passions and in being who they are. So many people merely settle in life, wearing whatever masks they feel they must to fit in. Let your children know how much you love them just the way they are and how much you value the unique qualities that make them who they are.

Notice what your kids are doing right, and let them know that you see it. Focus on their successes; make positive and encouraging comments rather than critical ones. We think that we need to guide our kids and teach them things, so our comments are too often couched as negatives: don't do this, don't act that way, don't forget to do this, and so on. But it's much more constructive and helpful to concentrate on the positives, and in doing so you're helping your children form a life-embracing attitude that can help them cope when they hit the inevitable obstacles. This goes for teachers and coaches too, whose support and encouraging words can literally change the lives of the kids who look up to them and hunger for their approval.

Kids are a gift—treat them that way. Keep your eye on the big picture, and let the small things go. Life is meant to be joyful. Make sure your kids see your joy and share it. Make great memories together—and be intentional about it.

If your child needs help, you're not alone. There are a lot of kids with anxiety, depression, and confidence issues, and many parents feel helpless and shut out. The key is finding a way to help parents improve communication with their kids and building a stronger connection so that when their kids need help, they come to their parents first.

Remember, your kids' perspective is different from yours. While it certainly matters what you say and how you say it, keep in mind that they may not hear it the way you intended. This works both ways; they may be expressing one thing to you, but you're hearing it in a wholly different way. "You never spend time with me!" can sound like an accusation and spur us to a defensive answer. But what they're really saying could be, "I'm feeling lonely and unlovable," or "My friends at school have turned against me. Can we talk about it?" Take a deep breath, listen, and then check in: "Is this what you're really worried about?" They may lash out at you about something that sounds trivial, but chances are that there's something much deeper that they're afraid of or stressed over, and that stress is spilling over into anger. Sometimes even they aren't clear on what it is that's making them so unhappy, and encouraging them to explore their feelings can help them uncover it and deal with it.

Listen without judging. That's the one piece of advice above all others that I'd like you to take away with you.

IF YOU'D LIKE TO LEARN MORE...

Visit my website at www.ConfidentHappyKids.com. You'll find some great free resources there to help you and your child, from meditations to tips on building confident kids.

I work with parents who are

- feeling disconnected from their kids;

- having trouble communicating with their kids;

- tired of power struggles, battles, or their kids lashing out in anger;

- going through a separation or divorce or are blending families;

- dealing with a difficult situation like losing a parent or being diagnosed with a terminal illness;

- worried about their children/teens—whether their children/teens are having issues at school, being bullied or bullying, being angry, feeling anxious or depressed, or struggling with low self-esteem; and/or

- just wanting to have more fun as a family.

I work with children who

- are stressed, overwhelmed, or anxious;

- have low self-esteem;

- have been bullied;

- are depressed, suicidal, or cutting;

- are unhappy or lonely;

- need help setting healthy boundaries;

- have difficulty communicating their needs;

- are angry;

- are dealing with family problems, including parental separation or divorce;

- have issues at school; and

- are grieving.

I also work with both parents and kids to give them tools to cope with everyday life more easily and to help reduce feeling stressed or overwhelmed. If I can help you and your child, I'd love to hear from you.

9 781599 327181